SUPER-FUN
Reading & Writing
Skill Builders

50 Motivating Reproducibles
That Reach & Teach Every Learner!

SCHOLASTIC
PROFESSIONAL BOOKS

New York • Toronto • London • Auckland • Sydney • Mexico City • New Delhi • Hong Kong

Cover design by Mo Bing Chan

Cover illustration by Lori Osiecki

Interior design by Ellen Matlach Hassell for Boultinghouse & Boultinghouse, Inc.

Interior illustrations by Teresa Anderko, Heidi Chang, and Manuel Rivera

ISBN: 0-439-06065-6

Copyright © 1998 by Scholastic Inc.

Contents

Introduction

Make learning fun and kids will eat it up!

That's what we've done in *Super-Fun Reading and Writing Skill Builders*. The grammar, usage, mechanics, vocabulary, reading-comprehension, and reading-response activities in this book are so entertaining your students will clamor for seconds!

Here are a few of the things on the menu:

- **Grammar Cop** helps kids learn essential rules of grammar.

- **Finish Me! Stories** teach parts of speech.

- **Anagrams, Riddles,** and **Hink Pinks** fortify students' vocabularies.

- **Rebuses** tickle the funny bone as they build spelling skills.

- **Reading Comprehension Reproducibles** provide a leg up when it comes to test-taking.

- **Graphic Organizers** offer kids ready-to-go tools to organize their thoughts and respond in meaningful ways to the books they read.

Use these instant, irresistible activities anytime of the day—from morning jump-starts to end-of-the-day treats! Turn to them to teach essential rules of grammar, extend mini-lessons, enhance learning centers, or simply provide practice for kids struggling with a particular skill.

No matter how you decide to use them, we guarantee that even your choosiest students will enjoy—and benefit from—these tasty morsels!

—the editors

Grammar Cop
and the case of the missing capital letters

The person who wrote this letter didn't really understand the laws of capital letters. Can you help Grammar Cop find the mistakes?

Dear cinderella and Prince Charming,

there must be a terrible mistake! the stepsisters and I have not yet received an invitation to your wedding. i keep telling the stepsisters that the invitation will arrive soon. i'm getting worried that our invitation got lost. i hear you often have problems with the unicorns that deliver the palace mail.

I'm sure you intend to invite us! After all, you were always my special favorite. How i spoiled you! i let you do all the best chores around the house. are you still mad about that trip to disney world? i don't know how we could have forgotten you! anyway, florida is too hot in the summer.

so cinderella, dear, please send along another invitation as soon as you can. i know how busy you are in your new palace. if you need any cleaning help, i can send one of your stepsisters along. they both miss you so much!

Best wishes,

Your not really so wicked stepmother

Directions: Circle the letters that should have been capitalized. Hint: There are 19 mistakes.

Remember these basic laws of capital letters:

• **Names**
Always capitalize someone's proper name. (Example: **G**ina, **K**enneth, **T**yrone)

• **Places**
Always capitalize the name of the town, city, state, and country. (Example: I live in **O**rchard **B**each, **C**alifornia, which is in the **U**nited **S**tates.)

• **I**
Always capitalize the letter *I* when it stands for a person. (Example: **I** am in fourth grade, and **I**'m ten years old.)

• **First letter**
Always capitalize the first letter of the first word of a sentence.

Name _____

Grammar Cop
and the Apology of Goldilocks

Goldilocks feels guilty about messing up the home of the three bears. She wants to make it up to them. But she doesn't understand the laws of possessive words. Can you help Grammar Cop fill in the blanks?

Dear Mama Bear, Papa Bear, and Baby Bear,

I owe you guy☐ an apology. I didn't mean to get my germ☐ all over everyone☐ porridge and break Baby Bear☐ chair. I didn't say to myself, "I think I'll head to the bear☐ cottage and mess up their stuff." I had been hiking through the wood☐, gathering rock☐ for my science project. I had stuffed all the rocks into my jacket☐ pocket. When I sat down in Baby Bear☐ chair, the rock☐ weight caused me to crush the chair.

To make it up to you, I would like you to come to my family☐ house for dinner. I have a new chair for Baby Bear. (I used all my baby-sitting money to pay for it.) Please let me know if you can come.

Love,

Goldilocks

P.S. I'll be serving some of my parent☐ homemade honey.

Directions: Wherever you see a box, decide whether the word needs an **'s**, an **s'** or a plain **s**. Write your answer in the box.

Remember these basic laws of possessives:

• **Singular possessive (*'s*)** Use *'s* when you want to show that something belongs to someone or something. (Example: That is **Bozo's** clown wig.)

• **Plural possessive (*s'*)** Use *s'* when something belongs to more than one person. (Example: Those are the **clowns'** wigs.)

• **Plural noun (*s*)** Use a plain *s* when you simply want to show that there is more than one of something. (Example: There are lots of **clowns** in town. They are all wearing **wigs**.)

Name _____

Grammar Cop
and the Case of the Big Bad Wolf

The wolf from "Little Red Riding Hood" is trying to tell his side of the story. But he doesn't really understand the difference between *its* and *it's.* Can you help Grammar Cop fill in the blanks?

I'm the wolf from "Little Red Riding Hood." You probably know me as the guy who ate Grandma. I'm here to tell you [____] all a big lie.

Every bedtime story needs [____] bad guy. But I didn't eat Grandma. I didn't dress up in Grandma's nightgown and chase Little Red Riding Hood. I didn't get killed by a hunter. [____] a big mistake.

[____] very simple. I was walking through the woods. I saw a basket with [____] lid open. I peeked inside and saw some cookies. I took just one cookie.

All of a sudden, someone yelled, "Hey! Put that cookie back! [____] mine!"

I looked over, and there was a little girl wearing a red cape and hood. She ran over and started yelling at me. She looked so scary! So I dropped the cookie. [____] crumbs flew behind me. I ran all the way home.

Little Red Riding Hood was so mad about her cookie. She started telling everyone that I had tried to eat her up. [____] all lies. You have to believe me. So the next time someone tells you the story of "Little Red Riding Hood," tell my side of the story.

[____] the truth!

Directions: The word *its* or *it's* belongs in each of the boxes. Choose the correct word and write it in.

Remember these basic laws of *its* and *it's*:

• ***It's***

It's is a contraction of "it is." A contraction is made up of two words that are joined by an apostrophe. The apostrophe shows where one or more letters have been left out. (Example: **It's** time for lunch.)

• ***Its***

Its is the possessive form of "it." The word *its* shows that "it" owns something. (Example: The squirrel dropped **its** acorn.)

Name _____

Grammar Cop

and the Education of Snow White

Snow White has left the seven dwarfs' cottage. She wants to explain her disappearance, but she doesn't really understand the difference between *your* and *you're.* Can you help Grammar Cop fill in the blanks?

Dear Dwarfs,

    [ ] probably wondering why I left. I have to admit I have gotten tired of [ ] strange habits. It seems like if [ ] not sneezing, then [ ] sleeping or [ ] acting grumpy.

    Also, it turned out that the prince wasn't for me. As I said to him, "[ ] really nice, but I don't want to sit around [ ] castle all day while [ ] off slaying dragons."

    The other day, I took a good look in the mirror. Sure it said, "[ ] the fairest of them all." But it also said, "Plan for [ ] future. What about [ ] education? [ ] career?"

    That was it. "Snow," I said, "say good-bye to [ ] dwarfs. [ ] going back to school."

    I hope I haven't hurt [ ] feelings. I appreciate [ ] kindness. [ ] all very generous. But for now, [ ] on [ ] own.

                     [ ] friend,
                      Snow White

Directions: The word *your* or *you're* belongs in each of the boxes. Choose the correct word and write it in.

Remember these basic laws of *your* and *you're:*

• **Your**
Your is the possessive form of *you*. Use it when you are talking about something that belongs to the person with whom you are speaking. (Example: I really like **your** new jeans. Where did you get them?)

• **You're**
You're is a contraction of "you are." Here's a tip: Whenever you write *you're*, read over the sentence and substitute *you are* for *you're*. If the sentence makes sense, you've made the right choice. (Example: I always tell people that **you're** my best friend.)

Name _____

Grammar Cop
and the Case of the Worried Elf

Santa's head elf is worried. But he doesn't know the difference among *their, they're,* and *there.* Can you help him? Fill in the right word in the blanks.

Directions: The word *their, they're,* or *there* belongs in each of the boxes. Choose the correct word and write it in.

Dear Santa,

　　　　☐　　is a problem with some of the elves.

☐ acting very lazy. I know that Christmas isn't until the end of December. But the elves aren't ready. Many of them can't even find ☐ tools. I caught a group of doll-making elves playing with ☐ Barbies. I saw some of the candy makers having a sword fight with ☐ candy canes. I inspected ☐ sleeping area, and I must tell you it's a disgusting mess down ☐ . I found candy wrappers and soda cans everywhere.

　　Santa, I know that the elves are a good bunch. ☐ all very sweet and nice. But ☐ like a bunch of kids. We must ask them to improve ☐ work habits. We must make sure ☐ ready for the big day. We need to make them responsible for cleaning up all of ☐ garbage. Most of all, we must make them understand that ☐ Santa's elves! Let's hope they get the message.

Very sincerely
Rocko, your head elf

Remember these basic laws of *their, they're,* and *there:*

• *Their*
Their is the possessive form of *they.* You use it when you want to say that something belongs to a group of people. (Example: They went sledding, but they forgot **their** mittens.)

• *They're*
They're is a contraction of *they are.* (Example: Mindy and Jessica are best friends. **They're** always together.)

• *There*
There is a place. It is the opposite of *here.* (Example: Australia is far away. I wonder if I'll ever go **there**.) *There* is also a pronoun used to introduce a sentence. (Example: **There** is someone at the door.)

Name _____

Grammar Cop
and the Three Little Pigs' Day in Court

The Three Little Pigs are trying to prove their case against the Big Bad Wolf. But they don't know the rules for using quotation marks. Can you help Grammar Cop by adding the quotation marks in their story?

One day the Three Little Pigs—Hambone, Porky, and Daisy—agreed that Wolf had bothered them long enough. I hate to be a pig, Daisy said, but I think we should sue him.

A few weeks later, they went to court. The courtroom was packed with other animals.

What's the problem? asked the judge.

Wolf won't leave us alone, said Hambone. He keeps blowing down our houses.

Porky said, He turned my house into a pigsty!

The judge asked Wolf if the charges were true.

They're all hogwash, said Wolf. I'm not guilty.

The judge said that he didn't know *what* to believe. Do you have witnesses? he asked the pigs.

The pigs looked at the other animals for help. But they all said that they were scared of Wolf.

The pigs were losing hope when a flea jumped out of Wolf's fur. I saw everything, she said. The pigs are telling the truth. Wolf is a real beast!

What a relief, Daisy said. Maybe now we'll all live happily ever after!

Directions: Add quotation marks to the story.

Remember these basic laws for quotation marks:

• **Direct quotes**
Put quotation marks around words that someone is actually saying. (Example: "Are you positive," Bill's mother asked, "that you want to put turnips on your sandwich?")

• **Indirect quotes**
Don't put quotation marks around words that summarize what someone said. (Example: Bill said that he likes to eat turnips at every meal.) Tip: Phrases such as *said that* or *reported that* are often good clues that you don't need quotation marks.)

Name _____

Grammar Cop
and a Case of Monkey Business

An idiom is an expression that means something different
from what its words literally mean. For example, if you
have a frog in your throat, that doesn't mean that you
have swallowed a little green animal! It means your voice
is scratchy and you sound like a frog when you talk. Can
you help Grammar Cop understand the idioms below?

Directions: Circle the correct animals in the following idioms.
Then write what the idiom means. Check your answers in a dictionary.

1. raining (rats/cats) and (dogs/pigs)

_____

2. making a mountain out of a (mole/ant)hill

_____

3. a (fly/goat) in the ointment

_____

4. a (whale/fish) out of water

_____

5. (fox/wolf) in (sheep's/elephant's) clothing

_____

6. crying (alligator/crocodile) tears

_____

7. (bats/birds) in your belfry

_____

8. you can't make a silk purse out of a (cow's/sow's) ear

_____

9. (snake/rabbit) in the grass

_____

10. (ducks/birds) of a feather flock together

_____

Super-Fun Reading & Writing Skill Builders Scholastic Professional Books

Name _____

Grammar Cop

and the Case of the Emperor's New Clothes

The emperor doesn't know if he's coming or going! He doesn't know what he has done, what he is doing now, and what he will do later. Can you help Grammar Cop choose the right tense?

_____ **1.** There <u>will be</u> a big parade next week.

_____ **2.** I <u>have</u> nothing to wear.

_____ **3.** I <u>asked</u> the tailors to make me a new cloak.

_____ **4.** They <u>promised</u> to make the best cloak the villagers had ever seen.

_____ **5.** The tailors <u>are working</u> day and night cutting and sewing.

_____ **6.** The cloak <u>is finished</u>!

_____ **7.** I <u>tried</u> it on, and something was very strange . . .

_____ **8.** But the tailors assured me that the townspeople <u>will be amazed</u>.

_____ **9.** After the parade, all the people <u>said</u> they had never seen anything like my new cloak.

_____ **10.** I <u>tried</u> to find the tailors to thank them, but they had left town.

Directions: Decide whether each underlined verb is in the past, present, or future tense. Write it in the blank.

Remember these basic laws of tenses:

• Past
The past tense of a verb tells that something already happened. (Example: I **walked** to school this morning.)

• Present
The present tense of a verb tells that something is happening now. (Example: It **is raining** today.)

• Future
The future tense of a verb tells that something will happen in the future. (Example: Tomorrow I **will play** soccer.)

Don't read this story yet!
Give it to a partner and
ask him or her to tell you
the parts of speech under
the blanks below. You give
a word for each part of
speech, and your partner
writes it in the blank.
Then he or she writes the
words in the story and
reads the story aloud.

1. _____
   ADJECTIVE

2. _____
   PAST-TENSE VERB

3. _____
   ADJECTIVE

4. _____
   ADJECTIVE

5. _____
   YOUR LAST NAME

6. _____
   ADVERB

7. _____
   PLURAL NOUN

8. _____
   YOUR TEACHER'S NAME

9. _____
   NOUN

10. _____
    FOREIGN LANGUAGE

11. _____
    YOUR PRINCIPAL'S NAME

12. _____
    EXCLAMATION

13. _____
    ZOO ANIMAL

14. _____
    PLURAL NOUN

15. _____
    VERB

Go to the Head of the Class

Being back at school is _____. Today I
                                  1

_____ into class, _____ as ever.
        2   3

All the teachers were sitting at the kids' desks!

"Good morning, _____ _____!"
                        4   5

they hollered _____. "Teach us about
                      6

_____!"
        7

I tried to take roll call, but _____
                                              8

was reciting the Pledge of _____ in
                                      9

_____.
        10

_____ ran in apologizing,
        11

"_____! I'm sorry! My _____
        12   13

ate my homework."

"We're late for our field trip to the Museum of

_____," someone shouted.
        14

I could barely keep up. I hope to get to

_____ at my regular desk tomorrow.
        15

Name _____

Super Silly Circus

Don't read this story yet!
Give it to a partner and
ask him or her to tell you
the parts of speech under
the blanks below. You give
a word for each part of
speech, and your partner
writes it in the blank.
Then he or she writes the
words in the story and
reads the story aloud.

1. _____
   YOUR CITY

2. _____
   ADJECTIVE

3. _____
   YOUR LAST NAME

4. _____
   NOUN

5. _____
   ADJECTIVE

6. _____
   VERB + *ER*

7. _____
   ADVERB

8. _____
   VERB

9. _____
   NUMBER

10. _____
    PLURAL NOUN

11. _____
    NOUN

12. _____
    BODY PART

13. _____
    PLURAL NOUN

14. _____
    ADJECTIVE

15. _____
    ADJECTIVE ENDING IN *EST*

Over the summer, the circus came to

_____ . Not just any _____
         1   2

circus, it was the Ringling Brothers and Barnum and

_____ Circus! My favorite performer was
        3

the _____ tamer who was fearless and
              4

_____ . The tightrope _____
        5   6

teetered _____ above the stage,
                 7

looking like she was about to _____ .
                                            8

We saw a _____ -foot-tall man juggling
                 9

_____ while wearing a _____
       10   11

on his _____ . All day we ate
              12

_____ , peanuts, and popcorn
        13

until we felt _____ . It really was
                     14

the _____ show on earth!
            15

Name _____

My Life as a

_____
13

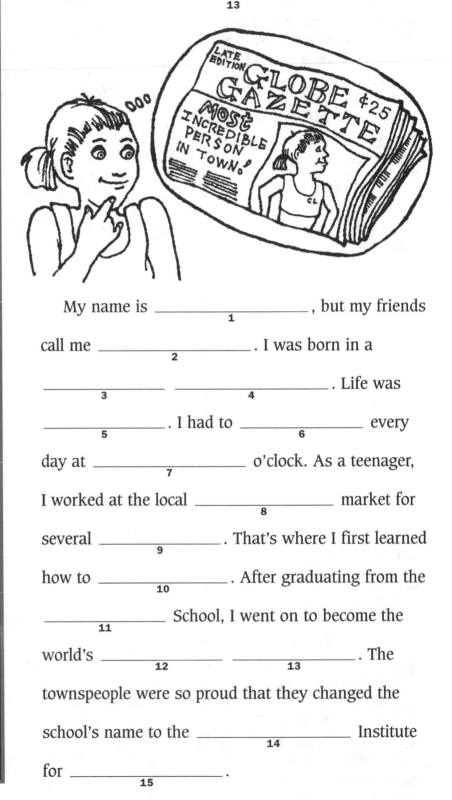

Don't read this story yet!
Give it to a partner and
ask him or her to tell you
the parts of speech under
the blanks below. You give
a word for each part of
speech, and your partner
writes it in the blank.
Then he or she writes the
words in the story and
reads the story aloud.

1. _____
   YOUR FULL NAME

2. _____
   NOUN

3. _____
   ADJECTIVE

4. _____
   ANIMAL HOME

5. _____
   ADJECTIVE

6. _____
   VERB

7. _____
   NUMBER

8. _____
   NOUN

9. _____
   PLURAL UNIT OF TIME

10. _____
    VERB

11. _____
    ADJECTIVE

12. _____
    ADJECTIVE ENDING IN *EST*

13. _____
    NOUN

14. _____
    YOUR LAST NAME

15. _____
    PLURAL NOUN

My name is _____ , but my friends
1

call me _____ . I was born in a
2

_____ _____ . Life was
3   4

_____ . I had to _____ every
5   6

day at _____ o'clock. As a teenager,
7

I worked at the local _____ market for
8

several _____ . That's where I first learned
9

how to _____ . After graduating from the
10

_____ School, I went on to become the
11

world's _____ _____ . The
12   13

townspeople were so proud that they changed the

school's name to the _____ Institute
14

for _____ .
15

Fright Night

Don't read this story yet! Give it to a partner and ask him or her to tell you the parts of speech under the blanks below. You give a word for each part of speech, and your partner writes it in the blank. Then he or she writes the words in the story and reads the story aloud.

1. _____
   ADJECTIVE

2. _____
   NOUN

3. _____
   BODY PART

4. _____
   FARM ANIMAL

5. _____
   PLURAL NOUN

6. _____
   PLURAL FOOD

7. _____
   YOUR NAME

8. _____
   VEGETABLE

9. _____
   ADJECTIVE

10. _____
    NOUN

11. _____
    PAST-TENSE VERB

12. _____
    PAST-TENSE VERB

13. _____
    PLACE

14. _____
    ADJECTIVE

Last time I went to a Halloween party, it was really _____ . One boy wore a
_____ on his _____ .
A girl was walking a _____ on a leash!
Another kid was putting _____ in his
mouth! We played games. First we bobbed for
_____ . Then we wanted to make a
_____ -o'-lantern, but we had no
pumpkin, just a _____ . We started to
carve it, and a _____ _____
jumped out! One of my friends _____ .
We all _____ away, but it followed us!
Then it swallowed my friends. I hid in the
_____ . When I came out, the thing had
left. I felt _____ that my friends were
gone. At least I got all the candy!

Gone to a Goofy Galaxy

Don't read this story yet! Give it to a partner and ask him or her to tell you the parts of speech under the blanks below. You give a word for each part of speech, and your partner writes it in the blank. Then he or she writes the words in the story and reads the story aloud.

1. _____
   ADJECTIVE

2. _____
   FRIEND'S NAME

3. _____
   NOUN

4. _____
   TEACHER'S LAST NAME

5. _____
   ADJECTIVE

6. _____
   ADJECTIVE

7. _____
   NOUN

8. _____
   VERB

9. _____
   BODY PART

10. _____
    NOUN

11. _____
    NOUN

12. _____
    YOUR TOWN OR CITY

13. _____
    FRIEND'S NAME

14. _____
    VERB

One _____ morning, _____
        1   2
and I were waiting for the school bus. Somehow, we

accidentally got on a flying _____ headed
                                    3
to the planet _____. When we landed,
                   4
we noticed the _____ sky. Soon, we were
                     5
surrounded by the _____ beings who lived
                         6
there. Each had a _____ where its head
                         7
should have been. I saw one creature teaching its

baby how to _____ with its nose!
                  8
   All of a sudden, two beings grabbed us by the

_____. They took us to the beautiful
      9
_____, where their leader lived. She
      10
gave me a _____ to bring back to
                 11
_____. I didn't have any gift to exchange,
      12
so I gave the leader _____ instead.
                            13
Finally, to celebrate our friendship, we all began

to _____.
        14

A Funny Fairy Tale

Don't read this story yet! Give it to a partner and ask him or her to tell you the parts of speech under the blanks below. You give a word for each part of speech, and your partner writes it in the blank. Then he or she writes the words in the story and reads the story aloud.

1. _____
   ADJECTIVE

2. _____
   NOUN

3. _____
   ADJECTIVE

4. _____
   ADJECTIVE

5. _____
   NOUN

6. _____
   PAST-TENSE VERB

7. _____
   ADJECTIVE ENDING IN Y

8. _____
   ADJECTIVE ENDING IN Y

9. _____
   TEACHER'S LAST NAME

10. _____
    NOUN

11. _____
    ADJECTIVE

12. _____
    ADJECTIVE

13. _____
    NUMBER

14. _____
    ADVERB

Once upon a time, a _____ princess
                        1
named Snow _____ lived with her
              2
_____ , wicked stepmother, the queen.
    3
One day the queen asked, "_____ mirror
                              4
on the _____ , who is the fairest of them
          5
all?" When the mirror answered "the princess,"
the queen flew into a rage. Snow got so scared that
she _____ and hid in the house of some
       6
dwarfs names Sneezy, Dopey, _____ ,
                                 7
_____ , and _____ . The clever
    8   9
queen disguised herself as an old _____
                                      10
and gave Snow a poisoned _____ apple.
                            11
Snow took one bite and fainted! Thank goodness a
handsome, _____ prince came by. He
             12
kissed Snow _____ times. Wouldn't you
               13
know it? They lived _____ ever after!
                        14

Name _____

Vote for Us!

Don't read this story yet! Give it to a partner and ask him or her to tell you the parts of speech under the blanks below. You give a word for each part of speech, and your partner writes it in the blank. Then he or she writes the words in the story and reads the story aloud.

1. _____
   YOUR NAME

2. _____
   ADJECTIVE

3. _____
   YOUR PARTNER'S NAME

4. _____
   NOUN

5. _____
   ADJECTIVE

6. _____
   ADJECTIVE ENDING IN *EST*

7. _____
   NOUN

8. _____
   NOUN

9. _____
   PLURAL NOUN

10. _____
    PLURAL ANIMAL

11. _____
    YOUR TEACHER'S NAME

12. _____
    VERB

13. _____
    NUMBER GREATER THAN 1

14. _____
    FAMOUS PERSON

15. _____
    ADJECTIVE

I'm _____ and I'm running for
                1

class president. My _____ running mate,
                              2

_____ , is running for class _____ .
        3   4

We have some pretty _____ ideas for
                                5

making our class the _____ in this school.
                                6

If elected, we'll quickly get a friendly _____
                                                    7

as our class mascot. Then we'll demand that

_____ class replace math class. We
        8

promise to get lots of really yummy _____
                                                9

and _____ served in the cafeteria.
            10

We'll also make sure that _____ lets
                                        11

us _____ instead of doing homework.
        12

Best of all, we pledge to recruit _____
                                              13

celebrities to join our class. So don't be surprised

to find _____ sitting next to you.
                14

If you want two fun and _____ leaders,
                                        15

vote for us!

Goofy Game Day

Don't read this story yet! Give it to a partner and ask him or her to tell you the parts of speech under the blanks below. You give a word for each part of speech, and your partner writes it in the blank. Then he or she writes the words in the story and reads the story aloud.

1. _____
   NOUN

2. _____
   FRIEND'S NAME

3. _____
   ADJECTIVE

4. _____
   NOUN

5. _____
   EXCLAMATION

6. _____
   PAST-TENSE VERB

7. _____
   TEACHER'S LAST NAME

8. _____
   PRINCIPAL'S LAST NAME

9. _____
   ADVERB

10. _____
    VERB ENIDNG IN _ING_

11. _____
    ADJECTIVE

12. _____
    ARTICLE OF CLOTHING

13. _____
    ADVERB

14. _____
    NOUN

15. _____
    PAST-TENSE VERB

Yesterday in gym class we were playing

_____ ball. _____
          1   2

was the captain of our _____ team,
                                 3

and my position was _____ back.
                              4

"33, 28, 57 _____!" The ball
                    5

_____ through the air. _____
        6   7

passed to _____, who fumbled
                    8

_____. I grabbed the ball and started
        9

_____. The _____ players
        10   11

came at me, trying to grab my _____.
                                            12

I ran as _____ as I could all the way to
              13

the _____ zone. I _____ a
          14   15

touchdown!

Name _____

Don't read this story yet!
Give it to a partner and
ask him or her to tell you
the parts of speech under
the blanks below. You give
a word for each part of
speech, and your partner
writes it in the blank.
Then he or she writes the
words in the story and
reads the story aloud.

1. _____
   FRIEND'S NAME

2. _____
   ADJECTIVE

3. _____
   ADVERB

4. _____
   NUMBER

5. _____
   PLURAL BODY PART

6. _____
   UNIT OF TIME

7. _____
   ADJECTIVE

8. _____
   NOUN

9. _____
   EXCLAMATION

10. _____
    PAST-TENSE VERB

11. _____
    VERB ENDING IN ING

12. _____
    YOUR STREET

13. _____
    ADJECTIVE

14. _____
    MOVIE STAR

Hollyweird

The book "_____ and the

_____ Mango" is being made into a
      2

movie. Guess who is playing the mango? I am and

_____ ! My costume is _____
      3   4

feet wide, and just my _____ stick out
                              5

at the bottom. The first _____ of
                                6

filming was a disaster. When the _____
                                          7

crew pushed me onto the set, I began rolling wildly.

Soon I was spinning like a _____ out of
                                    8

control. The director screamed, "_____!"
                                          9

as I _____ through a wall. I started
          10

_____ down _____ .
      11   12

_____ juice from my costume
      13

squirted everywhere. I finally landed—right on top

of _____ !
        14

22

Super-Fun Reading & Writing Skill Builders Scholastic Professional Books

Seasoned Greetings

Don't read this story yet!
Give it to a partner and
ask him or her to tell you
the parts of speech under
the blanks below. You give
a word for each part of
speech, and your partner
writes it in the blank.
Then he or she writes the
words in the story and
reads the story aloud.

1. _____
   FRIEND'S NAME

2. _____
   ADJECTIVE

3. _____
   ADJECTIVE

4. _____
   ADJECTIVE

5. _____
   NUMBER

6. _____
   NOUN

7. _____
   PLURAL FOOD

8. _____
   ANIMAL

9. _____
   BODY PART

10. _____
    ADJECTIVE

11. _____
    NOUN

12. _____
    ADJECTIVE

13. _____
    MOVIE STAR

14. _____
    ADVERB

15. _____
    YOUR NAME

Dear _____ ,
                1

_____ holidays to you! I hope
              2

the weather has been _____ and the food
                                  3

_____ . I also hope you get _____
        4   5

presents, especially that _____ you've
                                      6

been asking for!

   I've been very busy. I tried to learn how to cook

cranberry _____ , but they tasted terrible.
                   7

Even my pet _____ wouldn't eat them.
                      8

I also went sledding down Killer Mountain, and—

this is the bad part—I bruised my _____ .
                                              9

It really hurts.

   My parents have been just _____ ,
                                          10

though. They helped me build a _____
                                            11

in the backyard. It was really _____ and
                                            12

looks like _____ !
                  13

            Yours _____ ,
                           14

_____
        15

Name _____

Nothing to Sneeze At!

Don't read this story yet!
Give it to a partner and
ask him or her to tell you
the parts of speech under
the blanks below. You give
a word for each part of
speech, and your partner
writes it in the blank.
Then he or she writes the
words in the story and
reads the story aloud.

1. _____
   ADJECTIVE

2. _____
   ADJECTIVE

3. _____
   VERB

4. _____
   ADVERB

5. _____
   NOUN

6. _____
   NOUN

7. _____
   ADJECTIVE

8. _____
   VERB ENDING IN *ING*

9. _____
   NOUN

10. _____
    NOUN

11. _____
    NUMBER

12. _____
    NOUN

13. _____
    NOUN

14. _____
    OCCUPATION

Be _____, everyone! Winter is flu

season. Take care of yourself so you don't get

_____. Whenever you _____

outside, make sure you are dressed _____.

Button up your _____, and always wear

a _____ to keep warm. Be sure not to go

out when your hair is _____.

    You can tell you are getting sick when your

nose starts _____ and you have a

_____ache. If you think you have a

fever, take your temperature. Put a thermometer

in your _____ and leave it there for

_____ minutes. It's also a good idea

to eat lots of _____ noodle soup.

Remember, a _____ a day keeps the

_____ away!

Name _____

Finish Me!
Story

Happy New You!

Don't read this story yet!
Give it to a partner and
ask him or her to tell you
the parts of speech under
the blanks below. You give
a word for each part of
speech, and your partner
writes it in the blank.
Then he or she writes the
words in the story and
reads the story aloud.

1. _____
   ADJECTIVE ENDING IN *EST*

2. _____
   ADJECTIVE

3. _____
   PLURAL NOUN

4. _____
   ADJECTIVE

5. _____
   FAMOUS PERSON

6. _____
   PAST-TENSE VERB

7. _____
   ADJECTIVE

8. _____
   PLURAL NOUN

9. _____
   BODY PART

10. _____
    SILLY SOUND

11. _____
    ADVERB

12. _____
    ADVERB

13. _____
    ADJECTIVE

14. _____
    PLURAL NOUN

15. _____
    ADJECTIVE

I just made the _____ New Year's
                        1

resolution ever! I promised to clean up my very

_____ room. I started under my bed,
       2

where I found some smelly _____ . I also
                                   3

found my long-lost collection of _____
                                          4

_____ posters. I _____ for joy!
      5   6

I shoved them all in my closet, which got so full

that a box of _____ _____
                      7   8

fell on my _____ . " _____ ,"
                   9   10

I muttered _____ . I took everything out
                  11

and tried to stuff it _____ into my dresser.
                              12

Well, the dresser was full of _____
                                       13

_____ . What could I do but put
       14

everything in the only space left—under my bed.

See, keeping resolutions isn't hard at all when

you're as _____ as I am!
                  15

Name _____

Goose on the Loose

Don't read this story yet!
Give it to a partner and
ask him or her to tell you
the parts of speech under
the blanks below. You give
a word for each part of
speech, and your partner
writes it in the blank.
Then he or she writes the
words in the story and
reads the story aloud.

1. _____
   FRIEND'S NAME

2. _____
   COLOR

3. _____
   NOUN

4. _____
   ADJECTIVE

5. _____
   ADJECTIVE

6. _____
   PLURAL INSECT

7. _____
   VERB

8. _____
   VERB

9. _____
   VERB

10. _____
    ADJECTIVE

11. _____
    NUMBER

12. _____
    NOUN

13. _____
    NOUN

14. _____
    ADJECTIVE

15. _____
    FRIEND'S NAME

My friend _____ must be the great-

great-great-great-grandchild of Mother Goose.

My friend had a party last week. Besides me, the

guests were Little Boy _____, Peter Peter

_____ Eater, and a _____

woman who lived in a shoe. For dinner, we had

four and twenty _____ _____

baked in a pie. When the pie was opened, we all

began to _____. Then we played games

like _____-around-a-rosy and here we

_____ round the _____ berry

bush. We sang a song of _____ pence

and danced to tunes like "Rock-a-bye Baby, on

the _____ Top" and "Twinkle, Twinkle,

Little _____." The party ended after three

_____ mice ran by and _____

jumped over the moon.

Super-Fun Reading & Writing Skill Builders Scholastic Professional Books

Name _____

Don't read this story yet! Give it to a partner and ask him or her to tell you the parts of speech under the blanks below. You give a word for each part of speech, and your partner writes it in the blank. Then he or she writes the words in the story and reads the story aloud.

1. _____
   ADJECTIVE ENDING IN *EST*

2. _____
   ADJECTIVE

3. _____
   NOUN

4. _____
   NOUN

5. _____
   PLURAL ARTICLE OF CLOTHING

6. _____
   VERB

7. _____
   ADJECTIVE

8. _____
   NOUN

9. _____
   ADVERB

10. _____
    ANIMAL

11. _____
    PAST-TENSE VERB

12. _____
    ADJECTIVE

13. _____
    ADVERB

14. _____
    ADJECTIVE

Downhill Disaster

For winter break I had the

_____ vacation! We went skiing on
        1

Mount _____ _____ . I took
            2   3

the _____ lift straight to the top. My
            4

_____ were on, my goggles were in
        5

place, and I was ready to _____ . The
                                  6

snow was perfectly _____ , so I started
                            7

going really fast. Soon, I was zooming down the

mountain faster than a speeding _____ .
                                          8

I couldn't stop! _____ , I tried to grab
                        9

onto a tree, but then a _____ jumped
                                10

onto the back of my skis. We _____ to
                                     11

the ground and started tumbling and rolling,

turning into a giant _____ snowball!
                            12

At the bottom, we crashed into the lodge and

landed _____ , right in front of the
            13

fireplace. What a _____ trip!
                        14

Don't read this story yet! Give it to a partner and ask him or her to tell you the parts of speech under the blanks below. You give a word for each part of speech, and your partner writes it in the blank. Then he or she writes the words in the story and reads the story aloud.

1. _____
   FRIEND'S NAME

2. _____
   PLURAL UNIT OF TIME

3. _____
   ADJECTIVE

4. _____
   VERB ENDING IN *ING*

5. _____
   ADJECTIVE

6. _____
   ADJECTIVE ENDING IN *EST*

7. _____
   BODY PART

8. _____
   CELEBRITY'S LAST NAME

9. _____
   NOUN

10. _____
    PLURAL NOUN

11. _____
    ADVERB

12. _____
    ADJECTIVE

13. _____
    ADJECTIVE ENDING IN *ER*

14. _____
    VERB

Oh, My Aching Heart!

Dear _____,
          1

I have watched you from afar for many

_____ now. I can be silent no longer.
          2

The time has come to tell you how I feel. I think

you're really smart and _____ .
                                3

Whenever you are _____ near me in
                          4

class, I feel _____ inside. I think you
                    5

might be the _____ person I have ever
                    6

met. You are the apple of my _____ .
                                        7

   If you want to find out who I am, meet me at 3:30

behind Principal _____ 's office. I'll be the
                        8

one wearing the _____ on my head. Until
                        9

then, please accept this bunch of _____ as
                                            10

a sign of my affection.

                    Yours _____ ,
                                11

        Your _____ admirer
                    12

P.S. It is _____ to _____ and
                13   14

lose than never to love at all.

Name _____

Jungle Fever

Don't read this story yet! Give it to a partner and ask him or her to tell you the parts of speech under the blanks below. You give a word for each part of speech, and your partner writes it in the blank. Then he or she writes the words in the story and reads the story aloud.

1. _____
   PAST-TENSE VERB

2. _____
   PIECE OF CLOTHING

3. _____
   PAST-TENSE VERB

4. _____
   ADJECTIVE

5. _____
   NUMBER

6. _____
   ADJECTIVE

7. _____
   ADJECTIVE

8. _____
   PLURAL NOUN

9. _____
   PLURAL BODY PART

10. _____
    ADVERB

11. _____
    TEAM SPORT

12. _____
    FRIEND'S NAME

13. _____
    PIECE OF SPORTS EQUIPMENT

14. _____
    ADJECTIVE

I _____ up this morning and saw a
     1

lion wearing my _____ . I thought I was
                   2

dreaming, so I _____ my eyes. Suddenly,
                 3

a _____ noise came from the kitchen.
    4

_____ monkeys and a _____
     5   6

rhinoceros were sitting on top of the kitchen table

eating _____ _____ .
          7   8

"We brush our _____ after every meal,"
                 9

they said _____ . I looked outside and
            10

saw elephants playing _____ using
                        11

_____ as the _____ !
     12   13

Now I know the true _____ meaning of,
                       14

"It's a jungle out there!"

Don't read this story yet!
Give it to a partner and
ask him or her to tell you
the parts of speech under
the blanks below. You give
a word for each part of
speech, and your partner
writes it in the blank.
Then he or she writes the
words in the story and
reads the story aloud.

1. _____
   FRIEND'S NAME

2. _____
   ADJECTIVE

3. _____
   YOUR TOWN

4. _____
   FRIEND'S NAME

5. _____
   NOUN

6. _____
   ANIMAL

7. _____
   ADJECTIVE

8. _____
   NOUN

9. _____
   VERB

10. _____
    NOUN

11. _____
    ADJECTIVE

12. _____
    FRIEND'S NAME

13. _____
    ADJECTIVE

14. _____
    VERB

15. _____
    NOUN

Two at the Zoo

The whole thing was an accident. My friend

_____ and I just wanted to spend a
        1

_____ day at the _____ Zoo.
        2   3

Who knew that _____ would slip
                        4

on a _____ and bump into the
           5

_____ cage? The door sprang open, and
        6

the _____ creature inside, which was
          7

eating a _____ , ran out of the cage. It
              8

went nuts! I've never seen an animal _____
                                              9

like that before! The zookeeper came out with a giant

_____ to catch the _____
        10   11

beast. The zookeeper's eyesight wasn't good. He

caught _____ instead. Don't worry—
            12

my friend now lives in a _____ cage
                                13

and can _____ all day long, or even play
              14

with a _____ .
            15

Don't read this story yet! Give it to a partner and ask him or her to tell you the parts of speech under the blanks below. You give a word for each part of speech, and your partner writes it in the blank. Then he or she writes the words in the story and reads the story aloud.

1. _____
   ADVERB

2. _____
   YOUR TEACHER'S NAME

3. _____
   ADVERB

4. _____
   FRIEND'S NAME

5. _____
   NOUN

6. _____
   YOUR PRINCIPAL'S NAME

7. _____
   NOUN

8. _____
   ADJECTIVE

9. _____
   PLURAL FRUIT

10. _____
    PLURAL NOUN

11. _____
    PLURAL NOUN

12. _____
    FEMALE MOVIE STAR

13. _____
    PAST-TENSE VERB

14. _____
    ADJECTIVE

Appetite for April Fools

All morning on April 1st, we tried to play tricks on our teacher, who only said _____, "Just
                                                                            1
you wait."

At lunchtime, _____ yelled, "Food fight!"
                       2
_____, _____ threw a
       3   4
_____ cream pie that way. The teacher
       5
ducked, and the pie hit _____ in the face!
                                6
"Yee ha!" the principal yelled and threw a tray of

spaghetti and _____ balls! Before long,
                      7
_____ eggs and ham were flying! The janitor
       8
started throwing very ripe _____. Soon, we
                                    9
were covered with macaroni and _____ or had
                                        10
peanut butter and _____ coming out of our ears.
                          11
Finally, _____, our principal's mom,
                 12
_____ in. When _____ sauce hit
       13   14
her in the nose, she hollered, "ENOUGH!" The fight was

over. Even principals have to listen to their mothers.

Name _____

Don't read this story yet! Give it to a partner and ask him or her to tell you the parts of speech under the blanks below. You give a word for each part of speech, and your partner writes it in the blank. Then he or she writes the words in the story and reads the story aloud.

1. _____
   ADJECTIVE

2. _____
   ANIMAL

3. _____
   BODY PART

4. _____
   LIQUID

5. _____
   PLURAL NOUN

6. _____
   ADJECTIVE

7. _____
   NOUN

8. _____
   ADJECTIVE

9. _____
   NOUN

10. _____
    ADJECTIVE

11. _____
    VERB ENDING IN *ING*

12. _____
    EXCLAMATION

13. _____
    NUMBER

14. _____
    VERB ENDING IN *ING*

15. _____
    NOUN

My Summer Vacation

What a _____ summer I had at Camp
            1

_____ _____! I played tricks
      2   3

on everyone. Once, I replaced everyone's shampoo

with _____. Next, I put big _____
          4   5

in their backpacks and daddy _____ legs
                                        6

in their food! But then the tables turned. One night

after we told spooky _____ stories, I fell
                              7

asleep feeling scared and _____. A sound
                                    8

like a loud _____ woke me. I thought I
                  9

saw a _____ ghost _____
              10   11

toward me! You could hear me screaming

"_____!" from _____ miles
      12   13

away! Someone turned on a flashlight, and I saw

everyone _____ and laughing. The ghost
              14

was a _____ flapping in the wind. The
              15

joke was on me.

Attack of the Massive Melon!

Don't read this story yet! Give it to a partner and ask him or her to tell you the parts of speech under the blanks below. You give a word for each part of speech, and your partner writes it in the blank. Then he or she writes the words in the story and reads the story aloud.

1. _____
   ADJECTIVE ENDING IN *EST*

2. _____
   NOUN

3. _____
   PLURAL NOUN

4. _____
   ADJECTIVE

5. _____
   NOUN

6. _____
   VERB ENDING IN *ING*

7. _____
   FAMOUS PERSON

8. _____
   ADJECTIVE

9. _____
   ADVERB

10. _____
    NOUN

11. _____
    FAVORITE FOOD

12. _____
    NUMBER

13. _____
    BODY PART

14. _____
    VERB

I decided that I was going to grow

the _____ garden in the world. I used a
            1

_____ to dig holes in the backyard, then I
       2

spread seeds and _____ all around. Pretty
                         3

soon, my garden started looking _____ . I had
                                        4

planted _____ seeds, but a watermelon
              5

started _____ out of the ground! It grew
              6

and grew. This watermelon became bigger than

_____ ! Mom said we should eat it before
       7

it turned _____ . So every day I climbed
                8

_____ up a _____ , then leaped
       9   10

to the top of the melon and cut off huge pieces.

We made watermelon shakes, peanut butter and

watermelon sandwiches, and _____ with
                                   11

watermelon sauce. I've eaten almost nothing but

melon for the last _____ months! Mom
                          12

said, "Don't look a gift horse in the _____ ."
                                             13

I sure learned a lesson: Don't bite off more than you

can _____ !
         14

Be a World Builder

The shapes below are building blocks. Cut out the shapes and build as many houses as you can. There is one rule: Each house must spell a word, using a base word (roof). But not every house has to look like the example. Some houses have two floors or no chimney. Keep a list of all the words you build.

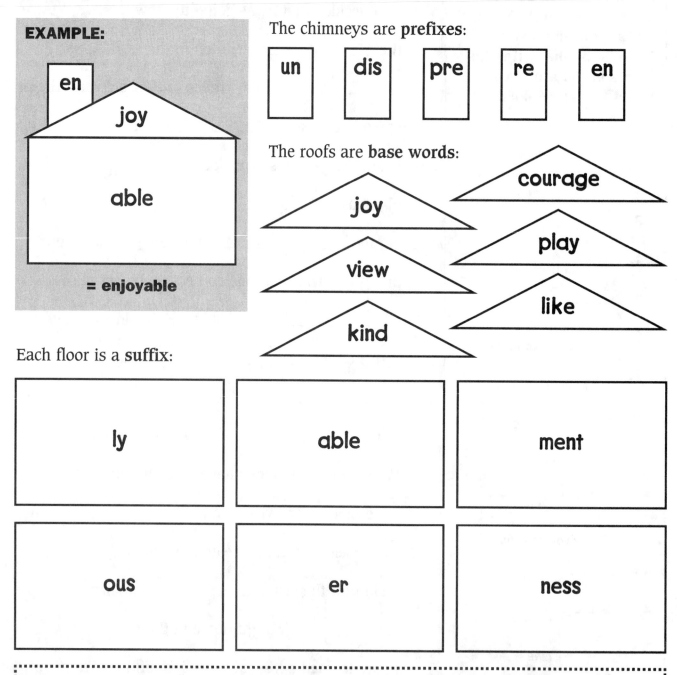

EXAMPLE:

en

joy

able

= enjoyable

The chimneys are **prefixes**:

un   dis   pre   re   en

The roofs are **base words**:

joy

view

kind

courage

play

like

Each floor is a **suffix**:

ly

able

ment

ous

er

ness

BONUS: Use at least five of your words to write a story about one of the houses you built. For example, you could write about what happens in the house called enjoyable.

It's GREEK to Me!

How is an astronaut like an ancient Greek?

a. They both wear long robes.

b. They both love Greek myths.

c. They both have Greek names.

THE ANSWER: c. Many English words contain Greek roots. Take the word *astronaut,* for example. *Astro* is Greek for "star." *Naut* means "sailor." So *astronaut* means "star sailor."

tele = at a distance
photo = light
sym = together
astro = star
micro = small
bio = life

phone = sound
phony = sound
pathy = feeling
graphy = writing
logy = word or study
scope = aim or target

DIRECTIONS: All of the word roots to the left are Greek. Take a root from column A and combine it with a root from column B to make eleven words.

1. _____
2. _____
3. _____
4. _____
5. _____
6. _____
7. _____
8. _____
9. _____
10. _____
11. _____

BONUS: Look up the following words in the dictionary: *decathlon, helicopter, kindergarten, parachute, porcupine, stegosaurus.* On a separate sheet of paper, write what their roots mean and what languages they come from.

Tasty Word Treats

After a long night of trick or treating, it's fun to unload your sack and see what's inside. The three candies below are full of **prefixes, base words,** and **suffixes.** Take one part from each candy to make a new word. Write the six words in the blanks.

Prefixes
Prefixes attach to the front of a word and give it a new meaning.

Base words
Base words can stand on their own.

Suffixes
Suffixes attach to the end of a word to change its meaning.

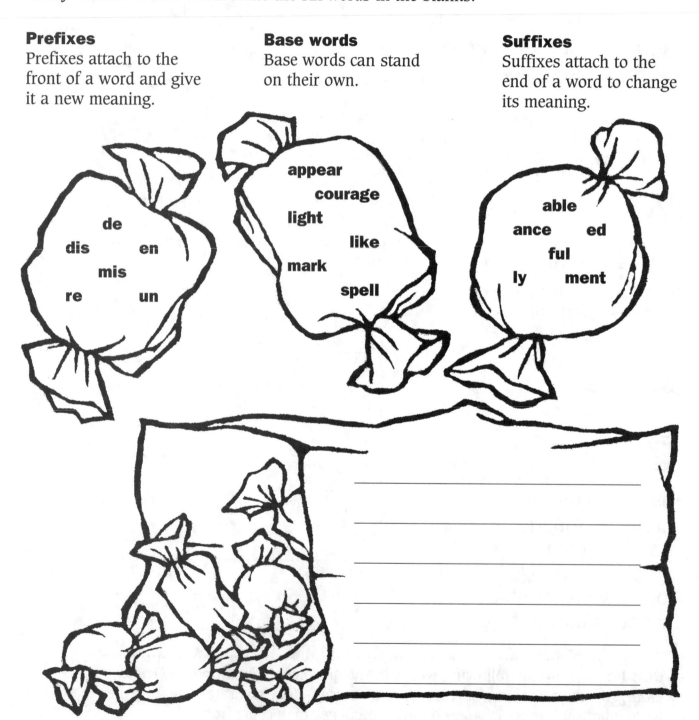

Super-Fun Reading & Writing Skill Builders Scholastic Professional Books

What's an Eye Hat?

Koko is a very special gorilla. She can communicate with her human friends. She understands more than 100 spoken words, and she is an expert (for an animal!) in sign language—both understanding signs and making them. Koko sometimes invents her own signs. She also puts together two or more words to describe a new word.

Draw a line from each word in the left column to Koko's definition in the right column.

1. mask	**a.** white-tiger
2. ring	**b.** bottle-match
3. zebra	**c.** bad-mad-you
4. monster	**d.** finger-bracelet
5. Pinocchio doll	**e.** surprise-devil
6. lighter	**f.** eye-hat
7. insult	**g.** my-cold-cup
8. ice-cream cone	**h.** elephant-baby

BONUS: Make up your own Koko-like compound words and challenge a friend to define them.

A Ram Sang (ANAGRAMS)

An **anagram** is a word or phrase made by rearranging the letters in another word or phrase. See how many anagrams you can make for each of the words below. (The first one is done for you.) Each word has at least two anagrams. Remember that some letters often go together, such as *st* or *ea*. Also, some letters can make more than one sound, for example the *c* in *cat* and *face*.

east	taps	acre
seat		
eats		
teas		
sate		

pools	tales	shape

snap	plate	times

BONUS: Find all the words you can using letters from *Tyrannosaurus rex*. For example, *run* and *sat*.

Riddle Recipe

Follow the recipe below to make up riddles
to challenge a friend.

1. Pick a subject: **pig**

2. Make a list of synonyms and
related words:

hog, swine, oink, ham, mud, snout

Hint: A thesaurus, a dictionary, an
encyclopedia, or a book about your
subject can help you find related
words.

3. Take any word from the list: **ham**

Drop off the first letter, leaving: **am**

4. List words that begin with **am**:
ambulance, amnesia

5. Put the **h** back on:
hambulance, hamnesia

These are your riddle answers.

6. Now make up your riddle using
the answer's definition:

**How do you take a pig
to the hospital?**

Answer: **in an hambulance**

**What do you call it when
a pig loses its memory?**

Answer: **hamnesia**

Now make up you own riddle.

_____

_____

_____

_____

_____

_____

_____

Hink Pink Riddle Recipe

Follow the recipe below to make up hink pinks to challenge a friend.

1. Make a list of pairs of words that rhyme. Choose one rhyming pair to be your riddle answer:

soggy froggy
glad lad
happy pappy

Hint: A rhyming dictionary is helpful.

2. Make up a riddle question. Make a list of words that have the same meaning as each word in your rhyming answer. (Words with the same meaning are called synonyms.) They do not have to rhyme. The synonyms will become part of your riddle question.

<u>**soggy**</u>   <u>**froggy**</u>
wet   amphibian
damp   toad

Hint: A book called a thesaurus is full of synonyms.

3. Pick one word from each column and make up your riddle question:

What do you call a wet amphibian?
or
What do you call a damp toad?

Answer: **a soggy froggy!**

Now make up you own hink pink.

_____
_____
_____
_____
_____
_____
_____
_____
_____
_____
_____
_____
_____
_____
_____
_____
_____
_____
_____
_____
_____
_____

A Beastly Puzzle

How many three- and four-letter animal names can you find in this puzzle? Words can be spelled by moving from letter to letter along the lines connecting the circles. For example, you can form the word DOG by starting at the D, moving southwest to the O and then north to the G. There are six more animals names in the puzzle.

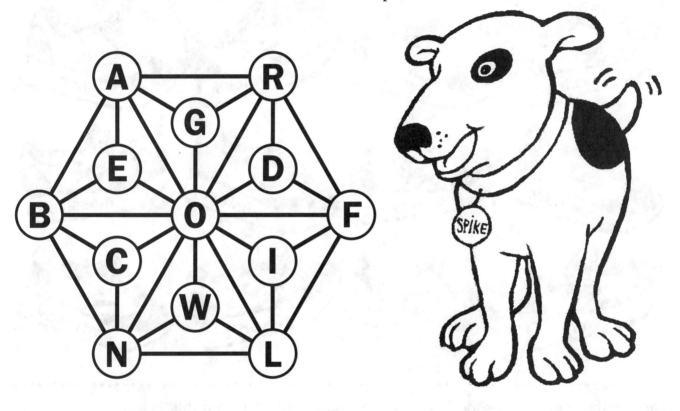

1. _____

2. _____

3. _____

4. _____

5. _____

6. _____

BONUS: There are lots of other words in this puzzle that aren't names of animals. Find as many as you can.

Two Left Feet

These shoes are all mixed up! You can pair them off. Each shoe contains a word that is a synonym for a word on another shoe. Synonyms are words that have the same or almost the same meaning. Put each pair of shoes together by coloring them the same color. Use a different color for each pair.

Lace up those synonym shoes! Each of the shoelaces has a word that is an antonym for a pair of shoes above. Antonyms are words that have the opposite meanings. Color each lace the same color as the pair of shoes that is its opposite.

BONUS: Create antonym *socks.* Challenge a friend to match them to the shoes.

Catch a Word Worm

Are you an early bird? Catch this worm! Starting from the top—the worm's head—connect the worm's body parts until you reach its tail. Don't leave any spaces. You can connect only parts that form words when stuck together. You can move left, right, down, or diagonally. The first two are done for you.

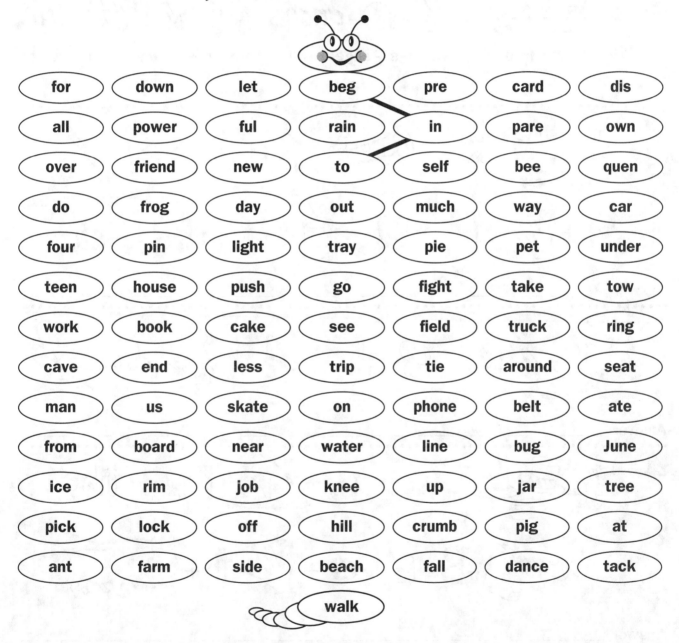

for	down	let	beg	pre	card	dis
all	power	ful	rain	in	pare	own
over	friend	new	to	self	bee	quen
do	frog	day	out	much	way	car
four	pin	light	tray	pie	pet	under
teen	house	push	go	fight	take	tow
work	book	cake	see	field	truck	ring
cave	end	less	trip	tie	around	seat
man	us	skate	on	phone	belt	ate
from	board	near	water	line	bug	June
ice	rim	job	knee	up	jar	tree
pick	lock	off	hill	crumb	pig	at
ant	farm	side	beach	fall	dance	tack

walk

BONUS: Make a list of all the other words you can find by connecting two body parts.

Tr +  This!

A rebus (re + ) is a sentence or phrase that uses letters, pictures, and symbols instead of words. Can you figure out each rebus below? The first one is done for you.

1

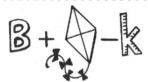  

h + gold – g = hold   y + orange – ange = your   horn – n + sevens – ven = horses

hold your horses

2

B + 🪁 – k   🔑 – S + FF   M + 🧹

t + ✋ – d   U   ch + 👠 – sh.

Answer _____

3

🦃 – 🔑 + N   🍀 – cl   A   🍝 – dlos 🍂.

Answer _____

4

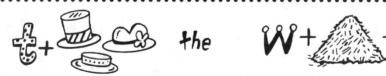

 C + 📖 – B + ie   cr + ✋ – th + 🐂.

Answer _____

BONUS: Make up a rebus for this sentence: *A bird in the hand is worth two in the bush.* Challenge a friend to solve it.

Super-Fun Reading & Writing Skill Builders Scholastic Professional Books

S + 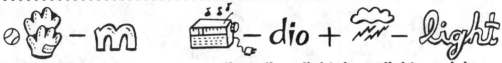 – i These!

A rebus (re + ) is a sentence or phrase that uses letters, pictures, and symbols instead of words. Can you figure out each rebus below? The first one is done for you. Hint: All of these rebuses contain animal words.

1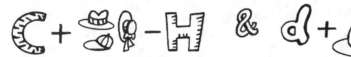

mitts – m = it's   radio – dio + lightning – light = raining

 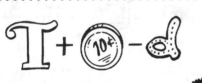

=c + hats – h = cat   d + frogs – fr = dogs

it's raining cats and dogs

2

Answer _____

3

Answer _____

4

Answer _____

BONUS: Make up a rebus for this sentence: *When I go to sleep, I like to count sheep.* Challenge a friend to solve it.

Say W +  ?

A rebus (re + ) is a sentence or phrase that uses letters, pictures, and symbols instead of words. Can you figure out each rebus below? The first one is done for you. Hint: All of these rebuses stand for famous sayings.

1

l + book – b = look   bee + four = before   you   sleep – s = leap

look before you leap

2

Answer _____

3

Answer _____

4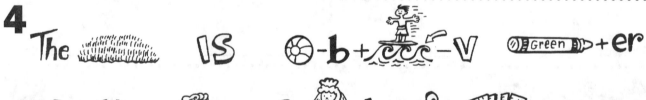

Answer _____

BONUS: Make up a rebus for this saying: *Don't count your chickens before they hatch.* Challenge a friend to solve it.

Super-Fun Reading & Writing Skill Builders Scholastic Professional Books

Name _____

America S + 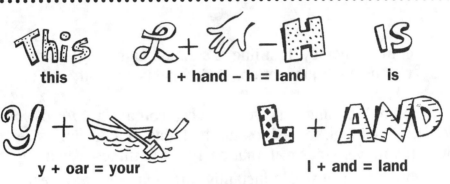 – r

A rebus (re + 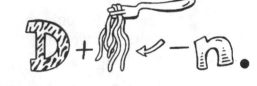) is a sentence or phrase that uses letters, pictures, and symbols instead of words. Can you figure out each rebus below? The first one is done for you. Hint: All of these rebuses stand for songs about America.

1

this   l + hand – h = land   is

y + oar = your   l + and = land

"This Land Is Your Land"

2

Answer _____

3

Answer _____

4

Answer _____

BONUS: Make up a rebus for this song: "You're a Grand Old Flag." Challenge a friend to solve it.

Zapped!

by Emily Costello

Getting struck by lightning is serious. Lightning-strike victims don't just get up, shake themselves off, and go home.

A bolt of lightning is powerful. It can contain *billions* of volts of electricity—enough to flash on all the lights in a medium-size town. If you were hit by all that energy, bad things would happen:

- Lightning's heat would instantly turn your sweat to steam. That steam could burn your skin and blow off your clothes and shoes.

- Electricity would race through your eyes, ears, nose, and mouth. It would cloud your vision and burst your eardrums.

- The explosive force of lightning could break your bones.

- Your muscles—including your heart—could stop working.

Each year, about 100 people in America die from lightning strikes. Another 400 Americans are struck but live. That sounds like a lot of people. But more than 270 million people live in the United States. That means that only one out of every 540,000 Americans get struck every year.

Want to be extra sure you're not one of them? Here are some ways to avoid getting zapped:

- Stay inside a solid building during severe thunderstorms. You'll also be safe in a car, as long as it isn't a convertible.

- Avoid metal pipes, appliances, and the telephone during a storm—don't take a shower or use your computer. Lightning can travel through metal and wires.

- If you must stay outside during a thunderstorm, keep away from high places, water, and tall objects. They attract lightning.

- If you can't find shelter, crouch down to make yourself as short as possible.

The best advice? The safest place to be during a thunderstorm in inside reading a good book.

Name _____

A Stormy Riddle

**Read the article on page 48. Then fill in the circle next to the best answer or ending
for each sentence. Use your answers to solve the riddle at the bottom of the page.**

1. This article is mostly about
   ○ A. how many people live in America.
   ○ B. driving a car in a storm.
   ○ C. what causes thunderstorms.
   ○ D. getting struck by lightning.

2. Lightning is powerful because it
   ○ E. comes from far away.
   ○ F. flashes.
   ○ G. makes rain fall.
   ○ H. contains a lot of energy.
   ○ I. comes in bolts.

3. Getting hit by lightning can
   ○ J. give you special powers.
   ○ K. seriously injure or kill you.
   ○ L. make you crave pizza.
   ○ M. make your hair curl.

4. If you are caught outside during a
   thunderstorm, you should
   ○ N. climb a mountain.
   ○ O. stay away from water.
   ○ P. stand under a tree.
   ○ Q. stand up as tall as you can.

5. Each year, lightning kills
   ○ R. 1 person.
   ○ S. 100 Americans.
   ○ T. 400 Americans.
   ○ U. 540,000 Americans.

6. Which is safest during a
   thunderstorm?
   ○ V. a swimming pool
   ○ W. a tall tower
   ○ X. a tent
   ○ Y. a solid building

7. In the article, it is clear that a
   convertible is a
   ○ Z. sofa.
   ○ A. truck.
   ○ B. toy car.
   ○ C. car with a top that folds down.
   ○ D. car that is broken.

8. In the United States, people are struck
   by lightning
   ○ E. rarely.
   ○ F. often.
   ○ G. only when they are in cars.
   ○ H. only when the sun is out.
   ○ I. only in cities.

9. The author of the article thinks it is
   ○ J. boring to watch lightning.
   ○ K. fun to get struck by lightning.
   ○ L. exciting to drive in a storm.
   ○ M. silly to be afraid of nature.
   ○ N. smart to be safe.

**Match the number under each line below to one of the questions you just answered.
Write the letter of your answer on the line to solve the riddle.**

Why did the man drive during a lightning storm?

His car ___ ___ ___ ___ ___ ___ ___ ___ ___ ___ ___ !
           9   8   8   1   8   1   5   2   4   7   3   5

To Bee or Not to Bee?

by Emily Costello

Where have all the honeybees gone? Last summer was less "buzzy" than usual. That's because not many honeybees were humming around. What happened? No one knows for sure, but scientists have several theories based on facts they've observed.

Some scientists think the cold winter last year killed a lot of the bees. Unlike most insects, bees usually live through the winter. They spend the cold months inside their warm hives, eating honey. Last winter was extra long and cold. The bees might have run out of food before spring.

But Michael Amspoker, a scientist and beekeeper, says that honeybees in America have a bigger problem than cold weather. A mite that is harmful to bees has invaded the United States from other parts of the world.

The mite, called the Varroa (va-RO-uh) mite, is a "flat little bean-shaped critter that lives on the bees' bodies," Amspoker says. The mites live by sucking the bees' body fluids. That weakens—and probably kills—the bees.

The mites are bad news for humans, too. Bees pollinate plants that produce many foods that humans eat. Bees also make honey and wax that humans use.

Scientists are fighting to save the honeybees. They have a secret weapon! A type of bee called the Yugo bee knows how to fight off the Varroa mites. The Yugo bees come from an area in Europe that was once Yugoslavia. They pick the mites up with their legs and crush them in their jaws.

Scientists will help American beekeepers introduce the Yugo queens into honeybee colonies here. Those Yugo queens should lay eggs that will hatch into a new generation of bees. Scientists hope that those baby bees will take after their mothers and know how to kill Varroa mites.

Will the scientists' experiment work? Wait until spring. Then see if you hear more buzzing.

A Buzzing Riddle

Read the article on page 50. Then fill in the circle next to the best answer or ending for each sentence. Use your answers to solve the riddle at the bottom of the page.

1. The main idea of the article is
   - ○ **A.** many honeybees have died because of a mite and a long winter.
   - ○ **B.** bees eat honey in the winter.
   - ○ **C.** some bees are moving to Yugoslavia.
   - ○ **D.** bees pollinate flowers and make wax.

2. It is clear that the word *theories* means
   - ○ **E.** guesses based on fact.
   - ○ **F.** facts.
   - ○ **G.** insects.
   - ○ **H.** problems based on fact.
   - ○ **I.** flowers.

3. Some of the information in the article comes from a
   - ○ **J.** farmer.
   - ○ **K.** cook.
   - ○ **L.** gardener.
   - ○ **M.** scientist.

4. Scientists want to fight the Varroa mite by
   - ○ **N.** gathering more honey.
   - ○ **O.** growing more foods that people eat.
   - ○ **P.** bringing the Yugo bee to America.
   - ○ **Q.** feeding the bees during winter.

5. Mites weaken bees by
   - ○ **R.** stealing their honey.
   - ○ **S.** sucking out their body fluids.
   - ○ **T.** crushing them in their jaws.
   - ○ **U.** killing flowers.

6. People need bees because bees
   - ○ **V.** are friendly insects.
   - ○ **W.** live in beehives.
   - ○ **X.** make a nice buzzing sound.
   - ○ **Y.** pollinate plants that humans eat.

7. The honeybees with mite troubles live
   - ○ **Z.** in Africa.
   - ○ **A.** in Europe.
   - ○ **B.** in America.
   - ○ **C.** under picnic tables.
   - ○ **D.** on mites.

8. Scientists hope that the Yugo bees brought to America will
   - ○ **E.** produce babies that know how to fight the Varroa mite.
   - ○ **F.** sting the honeybees.
   - ○ **G.** buzz loudly.
   - ○ **H.** help the honeybees build more hives.

Match the number under each line below to one of the questions you just answered. Write the letter of your answer on the line to solve the riddle.

What do you call a bee that can't make up its mind?

A ____ ____ ____ ____ ____ ____
  3   1   6   7   8   2

Lights, Camera, Yapping!

by Marie Morreale

Puppies, puppies everywhere! Jumping! Sniffing! Chewing! Barking! Yipping! Nipping! Acting!

Acting? Yes, acting!

Were there really 101 dalmatians in *101 Dalmatians*? No, there were more! During six months of filming, Gary Gero, the head animal trainer for the movie, and his team of 20 trainers had their hands full training four adult dalmatians and 230 puppies to be doggy actors. "Fortunately," Gary says, "dalmatians are very trainable."

Why so many puppies? The puppies grew so quickly that they were replaced every two to four weeks by new litters. That way, the dogs would look the same age throughout the movie. The puppies came from dalmatian breeders all over England, where the movie was filmed.

Gary and the trainers used a "food and fun" method to train the dogs. Each litter of 2 to 15 puppies had its own trainer. When the puppies did their scenes right, their trainers gave them bits of cooked chicken or dog cookies as treats. They also played with them. The rewards made the puppies want to follow instructions so they could get more food and fun!

The trainers also used the latest new training method—an electronic sound. The sound got the puppies' attention. The puppies soon learned that the sound meant they could earn tasty tidbits.

Gary has worked on many movies, including *Ace Ventura, Pet Detective.* He was excited to work with dalmatians. The breed is "very nice, sweet, affectionate, and well-tempered," he says. They are also very active. Still, Gary and the trainers got the puppies to finish their scenes. None of the puppies had an accident or got sick. If they had, they could have visited an animal hospital built just for the movie!

When the puppies finished their acting jobs, they went back to their breeders. Homes had already been found for each one. But how could the human crew that worked on the film bear to say good-bye to the puppies? Well, many crew members couldn't. They took home barking bundles of joy as a reminder of the film. Just ask Gary . . . if you can find him under the pile of his four adopted dalmatians!

A Puppy Puzzle

Read the article on page 52. Then fill in the circle next to the best answer or ending for each sentence. Use your answers to solve the riddle at the bottom of the page.

1. This article is mostly about
   - ○ A. what puppies like to eat.
   - ○ B. training puppies on the movie set of *101 Dalmatians.*
   - ○ C. how fast puppies grow.
   - ○ D. how to adopt dalmatian puppies.

2. Most of the article takes place
   - ○ E. on a movie set.
   - ○ F. at a veterinarian's office.
   - ○ G. at a farmhouse.
   - ○ H. at a pet store.

3. Which happens first in the article?
   - ○ I. Moviemakers get dalmatian puppies from breeders in England.
   - ○ J. The movie finishes filming.
   - ○ K. The puppies leave for their new homes.
   - ○ L. The puppies learn how to get rewards.

4. When the puppies followed instructions, they were
   - ○ M. rewarded with food and fun.
   - ○ N. sent to the animal hospital.
   - ○ O. adopted and left the movie set.
   - ○ P. replaced with a new litter.
   - ○ Q. given a pat on the head.

5. It is clear that the word *breed* in the article means a
   - ○ R. delicious food.
   - ○ S. game.
   - ○ T. kind of dog.
   - ○ U. movie starring animals.

6. The electronic sound made the puppies
   - ○ V. think it was time to go home.
   - ○ W. want to scratch fleas.
   - ○ X. sit up and beg.
   - ○ Y. think about getting food and fun.

7. You can tell that many of the crew members fell in love with the puppies because they
   - ○ Z. bought them presents.
   - ○ A. adopted some of them.
   - ○ B. took them for long walks.
   - ○ C. gave them chicken treats.

8. If Gary Gero is asked to work on another movie with dalmatians, he will probably
   - ○ D. say no.
   - ○ E. want to work with pigs instead.
   - ○ F. move to England.
   - ○ G. say yes, since dalmatians are sweet and easy to train.

Match the number under each line below to one of the questions you just answered. Write the letter of your answer on the line to solve the riddle.

What do you get when you cross a computer with a vicious dog?

A __ __ __ __ - __ __ __
   4 2 8 7   1 3 5 2

A Crayon Is Born

Would you like to have jungle green hair and atomic tangerine eyes? Hot magenta pants with a blizzard blue shirt?

You can! When you use crayons, you can color yourself any way you want.

Life wasn't always so colorful, though. A hundred years ago, all crayons were black. They were used in factories and shipyards to label crates and lumber. Kids couldn't use them because they were toxic.

Vivid Variety

Then a company called Binney & Smith had an idea. They decided to make Crayola crayons for kids and teachers to use in school. They figured out a formula that was safe, and they also decided to add color. The first box of eight Crayola crayons included black, brown, blue, red, purple, orange, yellow, and green. All the crayons were labeled by hand. The box cost five cents. The crayons were a huge hit!

Today, many companies make crayons, but Crayola is still the biggest. They take crayons *very* seriously, especially when it comes to color.

For example, Crayola has a team of seven chemists and chemical engineers who do nothing all day but develop new crayon colors. Their laboratory holds the unique, secret formula to every crayon color. They blend different colors to come up with new shades. Once the engineers discover a new color they like, they test it on hundreds of kids and parents to make sure it's really useful. Only then is a crayon ready for the box.

What's in a Name?

Then comes the hard part—figuring out what to name a new color. In 1993, Crayola introduced 16 new colors for its "Big Box" of 96 crayons. More than two million kids and adults wrote in with color name suggestions. Some winners were tickle me pink (bright pink), timber wolf (gray), purple mountains majesty (purple), tropical rainforest (bright green), granny smith apple (light green), and mauvelous (light pink).

Over the years, Crayola has changed some of its color names. In 1962, Crayola changed the name of its crayon color "flesh" to "peach." They recognized that not everyone's flesh is the same color.

Despite all the work Crayola puts into developing new colors, kids' tastes haven't changed much. Around the globe, kids still say that red and blue are their favorite crayon colors.

A Thief's Riddle

Read the article on page 54. Then fill in the circle next to the best answer or ending for each sentence. Use your answers to solve the riddle at the bottom of the page.

1. This article is mainly about
   ○ A. the people who name crayons.
   ○ B. how many crayons there are.
   ○ C. people who have green hair.
   ○ D. the making and naming of crayons.

2. In the third paragraph, what does the word *toxic* mean?
   ○ E. too big
   ○ F. black
   ○ G. broken
   ○ H. poisonous

3. Crayola changed the name of its crayon color "flesh" to "peach" because
   ○ I. not enough people were using "flesh."
   ○ J. not everyone's skin is the same shade.
   ○ K. a lot of people like peaches.
   ○ L. every year they change the names of all the colors.

4. What do engineers do when they discover a new color they like?
   ○ M. They throw away all the other colors.
   ○ N. They test it on kids and parents.
   ○ O. They draw pictures with it.
   ○ P. They have a party.

5. Which is **not** a new Crayola color name?
   ○ Q. timber wolf
   ○ R. hot chocolate
   ○ S. tickle me pink
   ○ T. tropical rainforest

6. The fourth paragraph is about
   ○ U. the first Crayola crayons.
   ○ V. how many crayon colors there are.
   ○ W. changing crayon names.
   ○ X. kids and parents.

7. Which sentence is an opinion?
   ○ Y. A hundred years ago, the only crayons were black.
   ○ Z. Some new crayon names were suggested by kids.
   ○ A. Red is the best color in the world.
   ○ B. Colors are developed by engineers.

8. Macaroni and cheese is a new crayon color. What colors do you think are in it?
   ○ C. blue and pink
   ○ D. red and purple
   ○ E. yellow and orange
   ○ F. brown and green

Match the number under each line below to one of the questions you just answered. Write the letter of your answer on the line to solve the riddle.

What's the best way to find crayon thieves?

Catch them ___ ___ ___ - ___ ___ ___ ___ ___!
           5   8   1   2   7   4   1   8   1

Kids in the Goldfields

by Liza Ketchum

Close your eyes and imagine that you can travel back in time. You're in California in 1850, just after the Gold Rush begins. You're still a child, but your life is completely different.

In the diggings, your family may have a tent, a rough shelter of pine boughs, or a tiny cabin. Your chores begin early in the morning when you haul water from the river, collect wood for the fire, or feed your family's animals before you watch your younger brothers or sisters. There is no school, but you will work hard all day long. Your parents need all the help you can give them.

You could help your father pan for gold or, if you're a boy, you may take his rifle and hunt for rabbits, quail, or squirrels. Girls might gather berries or wild edible plants in the forest.

If your mother runs a restaurant out of your family's tent, you may wait on tables or wash dishes. You might sing, dance, or play an instrument to entertain miners—and get paid in gold dust or coins. When the saloons are empty, you can run a wet pin along the cracks in the floorboards to pick up any gold dust spilled by miners the night before.

If you have any free time, you could play games with other kids. Or, if you're adventurous, you might sneak away to a Native American camp. The Pomo and Miwok Indians have lived in this area for generations. Maybe you could learn a few words of their languages and trade gold dust or coins for deerskin moccasins. You might also learn how these people's lives have changed now that miners have taken over the land where the Native Americans hunt and fish.

Later, you could pay a visit to some miners. Don't be surprised if they fuss over you and tell you stories, make you toys, or teach you to read. Most miners have left their families behind, and they miss their children.

Every once in a while, you might go to a dance nearby. If you're a girl, you'll be very popular. There are very few women in the diggings, so girls of all ages dance. Watch your bare feet around all those heavy boots!

What do you think? Would you enjoy the danger, excitement, hardship, and adventure of the California Gold Rush?

Strike It Rich!

Read the article on page 56. Then fill in the circle next to the best answer or ending for each sentence. Use your answers to solve the riddle at the bottom of the page.

1. What conclusion could you draw about the Gold Rush from this article?
   - ○ **A.** Everyone became very rich.
   - ○ **B.** Everyday life was not easy.
   - ○ **C.** Most miners brought their families with them.

2. Which sentence is an opinion?
   - ○ **D.** Some miners lived in tents.
   - ○ **E.** Mining for gold was a waste of time.
   - ○ **F.** Kids in the diggings worked hard.

3. From the article, you could guess that the word *edible* means
   - ○ **G.** safe to eat.
   - ○ **H.** delicious.
   - ○ **I.** cool and green.
   - ○ **J.** poisonous.

4. Pomo and Miwok are Native American
   - ○ **K.** authors.
   - ○ **L.** articles of clothing.
   - ○ **M.** canoes made of bark and wood.
   - ○ **N.** tribes.

5. According to the article, what chore might a kid living in the goldfields have had?
   - ○ **O.** vacuuming the carpets
   - ○ **P.** baby-sitting
   - ○ **Q.** mowing the yard

6. How did the miners affect the lives of Native Americans who lived nearby?
   - ○ **R.** Miners stole moccasins from them.
   - ○ **S.** Miners charged the Native Americans a toll to cross rivers.
   - ○ **T.** Miners stayed on their land.

7. Another good title for the article might be
   - ○ **U.** "A Kid's Guide to the Gold Rush."
   - ○ **V.** "California: Land of Gold and Sun."
   - ○ **W.** "Time Travel Back to the Civil War.

8. About how many years ago did the Gold Rush begin?
   - ○ **X.** 50
   - ○ **Y.** 100
   - ○ **Z.** 150
   - ○ **A.** 200

Match the number under each line below to one of the questions you just answered. Write the letter of your answer on the line to solve the riddle.

Where did the young dog sleep in the goldfields?

In a __ __ __   __ __ __ __ !
    5 7 5   6 2 4 6

Jackie Robinson: An American Hero

Back in 1947, many people in America discriminated against black people because of the color of their skin. In the South, blacks were forbidden by law to go to the same schools as whites, swim in the same pools, or even drink from the same water fountains.

Black baseball players such as Jackie Robinson, Satchel Paige, and Cool Papa Bell played in the so-called Negro Leagues, baseball leagues for blacks only. Like many Negro League stars, Robinson had the talent to play in the majors. He could hit with power, run the bases in a flash, and field ground balls with flawless grace. Fast and daring, Robinson had a talent for stealing bases. He even stole home a few times—a risky move that's rarely attempted.

One major league owner, Branch Rickey of the Brooklyn Dodgers, believed firmly that blacks should play in the majors. Beginning in 1945, he scouted the Negro Leagues for a star who could smash baseball's color barrier. After much searching, he chose Robinson.

Why Jackie Robinson? The 26-year-old star was mature and intelligent, and he had the will to succeed. He also had the courage and self-control not to respond to racist remarks by getting into fistfights.

Robinson played his first game with the Dodgers on April 15, 1947. All season, he endured racism wherever the Dodgers played. Fans cursed and spat at him. Others threatened to kill him. Opponents tried to knock him down on purpose.

Despite all the hardships, Robinson played brilliantly. He was named rookie of the year at the end of the season. By the time his ten-year playing career was over, Robinson's talent and courage had helped change many people's opinions of blacks.

In 1962, Jackie Robinson became the first black player inducted into the Baseball Hall of Fame. He died in 1972, at the age of 53.

A Baseball Riddle

Read the article on page 58. Then fill in the circle next to the best answer or ending for each sentence. Use your answers to solve the riddle at the bottom of the page.

1. This article is mostly about
   - ○ **A.** why Robinson stole a lot of bases.
   - ○ **B.** how baseball is segregated today.
   - ○ **C.** who played in the Negro Leagues.
   - ○ **D.** when the Dodgers moved to Los Angeles.
   - ○ **E.** how Jackie Robinson became the first black player in the major leagues.

2. In this article, the word *forbidden* means
   - ○ **F.** not allowed.
   - ○ **G.** decided.
   - ○ **H.** provided.
   - ○ **I.** written.

3. Branch Rickey hired a black player for the Dodgers because he
   - ○ **J.** was black himself.
   - ○ **K.** didn't have enough players.
   - ○ **L.** believed that black people should play in the major leagues.
   - ○ **M.** knew Jackie Robinson was a star.

4. What made Robinson's first year in the majors difficult?
   - ○ **N.** There were racist fans and opponents.
   - ○ **O.** He wasn't as talented as his white teammates.
   - ○ **P.** He was too old.
   - ○ **Q.** He got into fistfights.

5. Which happens *last* in the article?
   - ○ **R.** Branch Rickey scouts the Negro Leagues for a star to join the major leagues.
   - ○ **S.** Robinson is named rookie of the year.
   - ○ **T.** Fans are mean to Robinson during his first season in the majors.
   - ○ **U.** Robinson plays in the Negro Leagues.

6. Because Branch Rickey wanted to have a black player in the major leagues, he
   - ○ **V.** scouted the Negro Leagues.
   - ○ **W.** started the Negro Leagues.
   - ○ **X.** made Jackie Robinson rookie of the year.
   - ○ **Y.** bought the Brooklyn Dodgers.

7. According to the article, which would best describe Jackie Robinson?
   - ○ **Z.** strong and angry
   - ○ **A.** courageous and talented
   - ○ **B.** stubborn and immature
   - ○ **C.** fast and afraid

Match the number under each line below to one of the questions you just answered. Write the letter of your answer on the line to solve the riddle.

Why is a baseball field hot after a baseball game?

The __ __ __ __ __ __ __ __ __ __ __ __
   2 7 4 5   7 3 3   3 1 7 6 1

E. B. White: The Author Who Spun Charlotte's Web

One day, on a small farm in Maine, a man sat in a barn watching a large gray spider spin a web. The man was E. B. White. Andy, as White was called, thought that spiders were spectacular creatures. He thought that one day he might like to write a children's book about a spider.

But writing was hard work for Andy. He had written many articles and essays and poems. He had also written one children's book, *Stuart Little.*

But Andy could never just rush to turn an idea into an article or a book. He said that he needed to let his ideas "ripen."

So for years, Andy continued to think about writing a children's book about a spider. He did some of his best thinking while he meandered around his farm.

Once while he was cleaning his barn, he found a spider's egg sac. Andy wanted to see the eggs hatch. But he was scheduled to leave for a trip to New York City. So he found a small box and carefully placed the egg sac inside. When he got to his hotel, he put the box on the dresser. One morning he woke up, and there were hundreds of baby spiders scurrying across the dresser!

Years later, Andy finally began writing *Charlotte's Web,* the story of a spider named Charlotte and a pig named Wilbur. Andy created most of the book sitting by himself in the tiny boathouse of his farm. Sometimes he stopped writing and doodled pictures of spiders.

Andy always said that *Charlotte's Web* was more than just a children's story about animals. It was a timeless story about true friendship.

Super-Fun Reading & Writing Skill Builders Scholastic Professional Books

A Spider Riddle

Read the article on page 60. Then fill in the circle next to the best answer or ending for each sentence. Use your answers to solve the riddle at the bottom of the page.

1. The main idea of the article is
   ○ **A.** E. B. White loved spiders.
   ○ **B.** how E. B. White wrote *Charlotte's Web.*
   ○ **C.** E. B. White liked living on a farm.
   ○ **D.** why E. B. White was called Andy.

2. Andy's farm was located in
   ○ **E.** Maine.
   ○ **F.** Westchester County.
   ○ **G.** Canada.
   ○ **H.** New Jersey.

3. When Andy said he wanted his ideas to "ripen" before he wrote a book, he meant
   ○ **I.** he wanted them slowly to grow and improve.
   ○ **J.** he wanted them to happen quickly.
   ○ **K.** he waned to write them on fruit-scented paper.
   ○ **L.** he wanted to discuss them with his wife, Charlotte.

4. According to the article, Andy brought the spider's eggs to New York City because
   ○ **M.** he didn't want spiders living on his farm.
   ○ **N.** the mother spider had died.
   ○ **O.** he wanted to keep them safe.
   ○ **P.** he wanted to watch the eggs hatch.

5. Which is **not** a detail from the first paragraph?
   ○ **Q.** E. B. White sat in a barn.
   ○ **R.** Andy watched a spider spin a web.
   ○ **S.** He wanted to write about a spider.
   ○ **T.** Andy wrote *Stuart Little.*

6. Which sentence is an opinion?
   ○ **U.** Andy wrote many articles and poems.
   ○ **V.** Andy traveled to New York City.
   ○ **W.** *Charlotte's Web* is the best children's book ever written.
   ○ **X.** Spiders lay eggs.

7. According to the article, how did Andy feel about spiders?
   ○ **Y.** He enjoyed watching them.
   ○ **Z.** He was afraid of them.
   ○ **A.** He thought they were pests.
   ○ **B.** He collected them.

8. Andy wrote most of *Charlotte's Web* in
   ○ **C.** an office.
   ○ **D.** a boathouse.
   ○ **E.** pig Latin.

9. Andy said that *Charlotte's Web* was really about
   ○ **F.** true friendship.
   ○ **G.** the eating habits of spiders and pigs.
   ○ **H.** animal extinction.
   ○ **I.** war and peace.

Match the number under each line below to one of the questions you just answered. Write the letter of your answer on the line to solve the riddle.

What did the duck get when he stepped on a spider?

___ ___ ___ ___ ___ ___ ___ ___ ___ ___
 6   2   1   1   2   8   9   2   2   5

The Secret Soldier

A young soldier, Robert Shurtliff, lay dying in a hospital bed. He was too weak to speak or move. Two men stood over him.

"I think this young lad has passed away," one man said.

"I'll take his jacket and boots," said the other.

Robert gathered all of his strength to whisper, "I . . . I'm alive."

The doctor came running over as Robert fell into a coma. "We can save him," he said as he examined the young soldier. "Oh, my! He's a woman!"

It was true. The courageous soldier, Robert Shurtliff, was really Deborah Sampson. But who was she?

Deborah had grown up in Massachusetts, living as a servant. She dreamed of having great adventures.

The Revolutionary War began in 1775. The thirteen colonies of America were fighting to gain their independence from England. The American Army, led by General George Washington, needed many soldiers.

Women were forbidden from serving in the military. But Deborah had a plan. She wove her own suit and disguised herself as a man. Not even her own mother recognized her!

At the age of 21, dressed as a man, Deborah Sampson became a soldier. She called herself Robert Shurtliff.

Just like the other soldiers, Deborah was given a uniform, gun, and heavy knapsack. She went on long marches in the middle of winter. Sometimes she went for days without food. But she never complained. Everyone thought Robert Shurtliff was a very good soldier.

One day, during an attack, Deborah was shot in the neck and leg. Another soldier lifted Deborah onto his horse and rode her to the hospital. A doctor treated the wound on her neck and asked if she had any other injuries. There was blood dripping down into her boot, but Deborah lied and said no. She was afraid that if the doctor examined her leg, he would discover her secret. Using a pocket knife, Deborah carved the bullet out of her own leg. She continued to fight as a soldier.

After the war ended, Deborah got married and had children. But she still longed for adventure. So she put on her soldier's uniform and traveled around the country telling of her life as the young, brave soldier, Robert Shurtliff.

Name _____

How to Keep Your Facts Straight

Imagine that you have to write a report on secret soldier Deborah Sampson. This activity will help get your organized.

1. Read the article on page 62.

2. Look at the index cards below. The title on each card tells you what kind of information you should write on it.

3. Reread the article to find information that belongs on each card. Do one card at a time.

4. Write three facts on each index card.

The Revolutionary War

1.

2.

3.

How and Why Deborah Became a Soldier

1.

2.

3.

Deborah's Experiences in the War

1.

2.

3.

Words That Describe Deborah

1.

2.

3.

Super-Fun Reading & Writing Skill Builders Scholastic Professional Books

Name ____________________

Reading Response: Think While Reading

Pack Your Bags

Have you ever heard of an armchair traveler? That's someone who sits in a chair and reads all about a place without going there. You can be an armchair explorer! Think of a topic you really want to explore. Choose a book or two to read about the topic. Fill in the first two suitcases (K and W) before you read. Afterward, fill in the other two suitcases (L and S).

Topic ____________________

Book(s) I am reading ____________________

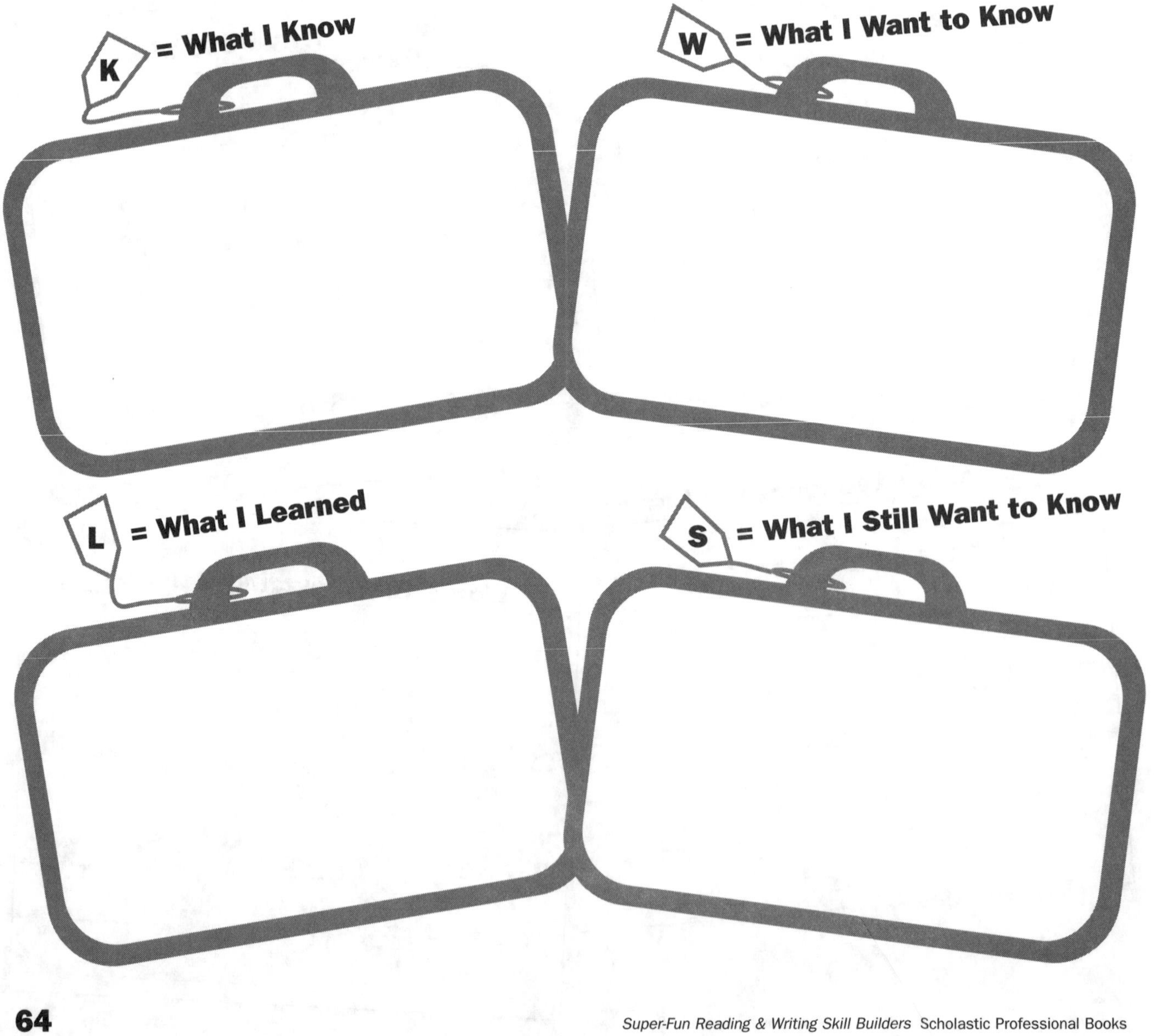

K = What I Know
W = What I Want to Know
L = What I Learned
S = What I Still Want to Know

Name ______________________________

Reading Response: Predicting/ Summarizing

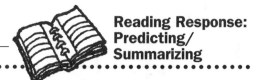

What Do You Think?

You've been waiting months for this book to appear on the library shelf. Now it's finally in. Wait just a minute more to fill out the left page of the book below before you start reading. Hint: Use the title, artwork, and chapter headings as clues.

Fill in the right side after you finish the book. Which of your predictions were correct? What surprised you about the book?

Title ______________________________

Author ______________________________

I Predict

The story is about:

____

____

____

____

____

This will happen in the book:

____

____

____

____

____

Now I Know

The story was about:

____

____

____

As I expected, this happened in the book:

____

____

____

This is what surprised me about the book:

____

____

____

Name _____

Build a Story Pyramid

After you read a story, you can build a story pyramid. The numbered directions below tell you how to fill in each level of the pyramid.

Title _____

Author _____

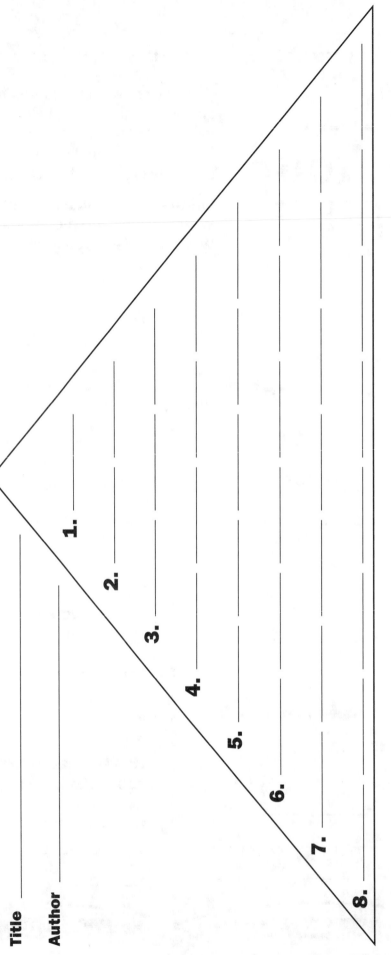

1.

2.

3.

4.

5.

6.

7.

8.

1. name of the main character
2. 2 words: describe the main character
3. 3 words: describe the setting
4. 4 words: state the main character's goal or problem
5. 5 words: describe an important event
6. 6 words: describe the conclusion
7. 7 words: describe your favorite part
8. 8 words: what would you tell others about the story?

Super-Fun Reading & Writing Skill Builders Scholastic Professional Books

Name ______________________________

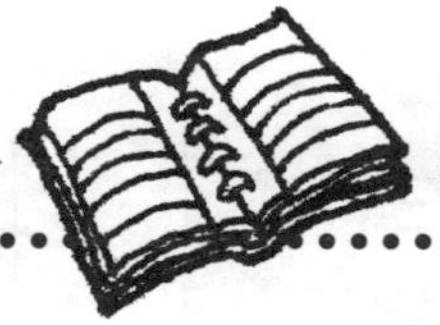

Sum It Up

Make a sum-it-up card for each article or book you read. Fill in the blanks. Use your three facts to write a summary. Then cut along the outside of the box, fold the box in half, and tape the edges together. Soon you will have an incredible collection of cards to show what you know!

✷ SUM IT UP ✷ SUM IT UP ✷ SUM IT UP ✷ SUM IT UP ✷ ✷ SUM IT UP ✷ SUM IT UP ✷ SUM IT UP ✷ SUM IT UP ✷

↑ TAPE ON THIS EDGE ↑

Title: ______________________________

Author: ______________________________

Three important facts:

1. ______________________________

____

____

2. ______________________________

____

____

3. ______________________________

____

____

Write a summary that tells the main idea.

Summary: ______________________________

____

____

____

____

____

____

____

____

____

Your name: ______________________________

↑ TAPE ON THIS EDGE ↑

✷ SUM IT UP ✷ SUM IT UP ✷ SUM IT UP ✷ SUM IT UP ✷ ✷ SUM IT UP ✷ SUM IT UP ✷ SUM IT UP ✷ SUM IT UP ✷

↑ FOLD ON DASHED LINE

Name _____

Story Pie

On scrap paper, make a list of the events in a story you read recently. In the story pie below, put the events in the order in which they happen. Put the first main event in piece 1. Tell how the story ends in piece 10.

Title _____

Author _____

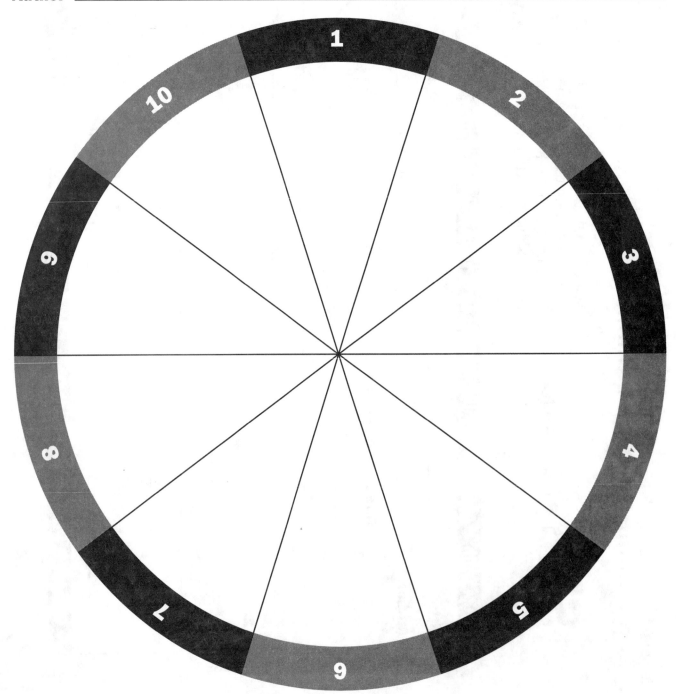

Name _____

Solving a Problem

Every story has a problem, no matter how small. Part of the fun of reading a story is finding out how the characters solve their problems. After you read a story, answer these questions.

Title _____

1. Tell the main problem in the story.

_____

_____

2. Tell the different things that the characters suggested to try to solve the problem.

_____

_____

_____

3. Tell how the problem was finally solved.

_____

_____

_____

4. Think of a different way you might have solved this problem.

_____

_____

_____

5. Would your solution to the problem have changed the story in any way? Explain.

_____

_____

_____

_____

Name _____

So That's the Reason!

A **cause** makes something happen. It answers the question "Why?" An **effect** is what happens as a result of a cause. Below, the **cause** is underlined in the top example and the **effect** in the bottom example.

<u>Pinocchio told a lie.</u> So his nose grew ten feet.

The circus master threw Pinocchio into the sea.
<u>As a result, he got swallowed by a giant sea monster.</u>

Think of important events in a story you have read. Come up with your own examples of cause and effect. Write a cause on the line next to each arrow. Write its effect on the target.

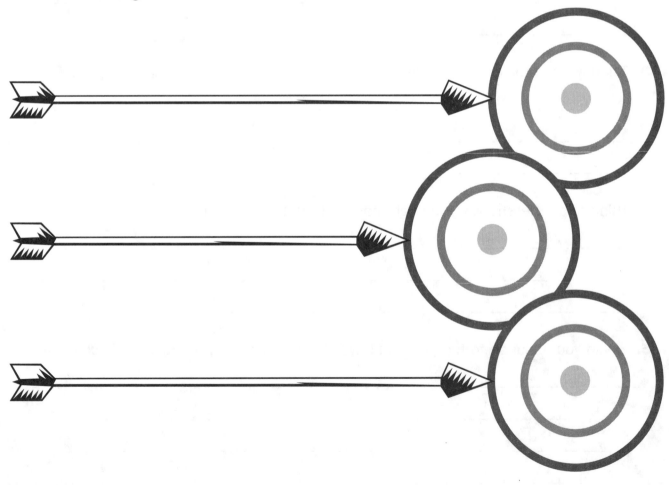

Super-Fun Reading & Writing Skill Builders Scholastic Professional Books

Name _____

Where's the Action?

In some books, characters travel to faraway places. In other books, people stick close to home. The action may take place in a school or on the main character's street.

On another sheet of paper, make a list of the places where things happen in a book you are reading. Draw a small picture to represent each place. Use the pictures to help you draw a map here, showing important places from the book.

A map of _____ **from** _____
(TITLE OF BOOK)

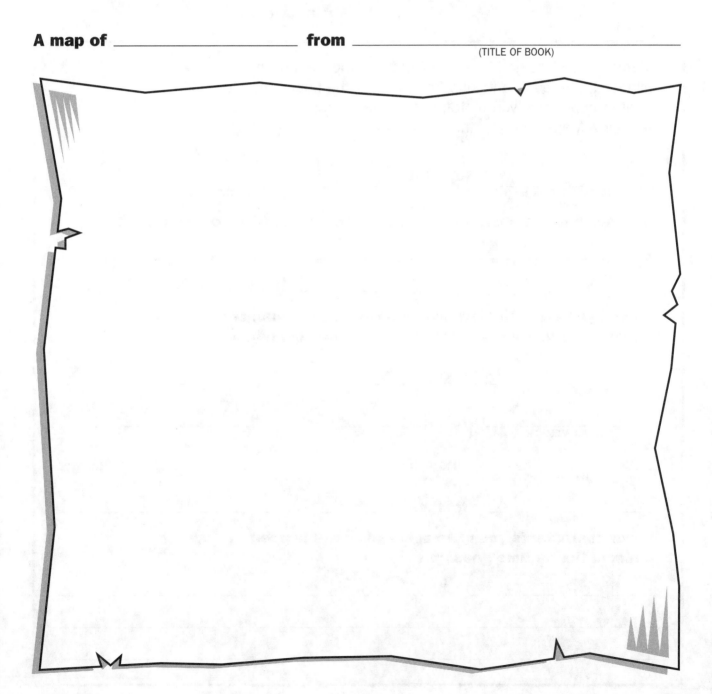

Name _____

Telling a Life Story

A biographer writes about someone else's life. A biographer may read about the person, talk with his or her family or friends, or visit important places where the person lived and worked. The biographer may even get a chance to interview the subject of the book.

Could a biographer write about someone who never lived? Yes—but only by using a lot of imagination! Try it. Choose an interesting character in a book you have read.

Directions: List some ideas and facts you know about the character's childhood, interests, and jobs from reading the book. Then, on another sheet of paper, use your notes about your character to write his or her biography. Make sure you think of a great title!

_____ **from** _____
(CHARACTER'S NAME)   (BOOK'S TITLE)

Write some notes about the places your character lives or travels.

_____

_____

Pretend you are interviewing people about the character.
Use your imagination and the facts you already know.

_____ **told me** _____
(FAMILY MEMBER)

_____ **told me** _____
(FAMILY MEMBER)

_____ **told me** _____
(FRIEND)

_____ **told me** _____
(FRIEND)

If your character is young, imagine what will happen
to him or her as time goes on.

_____

_____

_____

Name _____

Put Yourself in Someone Else's Shoes

Do you always agree with the decisions made or actions taken by characters in books? Think of a time you did not agree with a character. In the shoe on the left, write about the situation and what the character did. In the shoe on the right, write about what you would have done if you were the character. Why would you have done things another way?

Name _____

Want to Trade? Again!

Think of a character you would like to make a trading card about. On the front and back of the card below, write information about the character and draw or paste a picture of him or her.

↓ TAPE ON THIS EDGE ↓

✹ CHARACTER CARD ✹

Occupation: _____

Age: _____

Place of birth: _____

Favorite _____
YOU FILL IN

Most memorable adventure: _____

_____

Quote: _____

Two pieces of information: _____

_____

← FOLD ON DASHED LINE

✹ CHARACTER CARD ✹

Character's name: _____

Appeared in (title): _____

↑ TAPE ON THIS EDGE ↑

Super-Fun Reading & Writing Skill Builders Scholastic Professional Books

Name _____

Picture This!

Choose the illustrations from two books to compare and contrast. Write the title and illustrator of one book on the solid lines. Write the title and illustrator of the other book on the dashed lines. Write words and phrases that specifically describe each book's illustrations in the oval for that book. Write words and phrases that can describe *both* books' illustrations in the space where the ovals overlap.

Think about things like what kinds of colors the illustrator used, how the illustrations make you feel, and what materials the illustrator used to create the pictures.

Title _____

Illustrator _____

Title - - - - - - - - - - - - - -

Illustrator - - - - - - - - - - - -

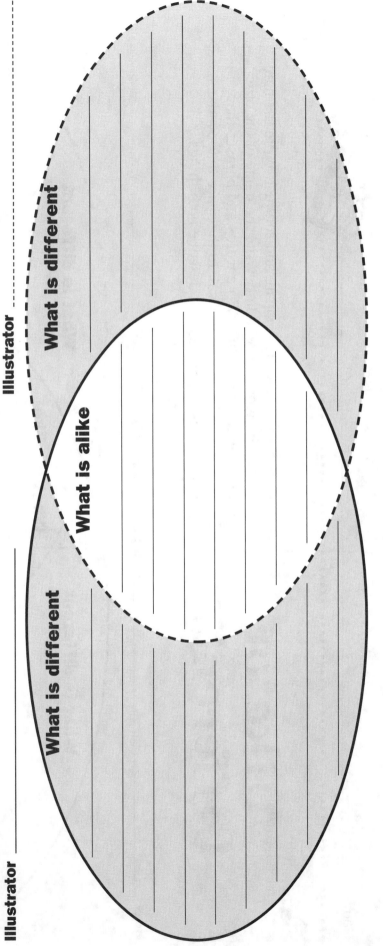

What is different

What is alike

What is different

**Reading Response:
Compare and
Contrast**

Alike or Different?

Choose two things to compare and contrast. Write the name of one thing on the solid line. Write the name of the other thing on the dotted line. Write words and phrases that describe each thing in its oval. In the space that overlaps, write words or phrases that describe both things.

How _____ **compares and contrasts with** ----------------

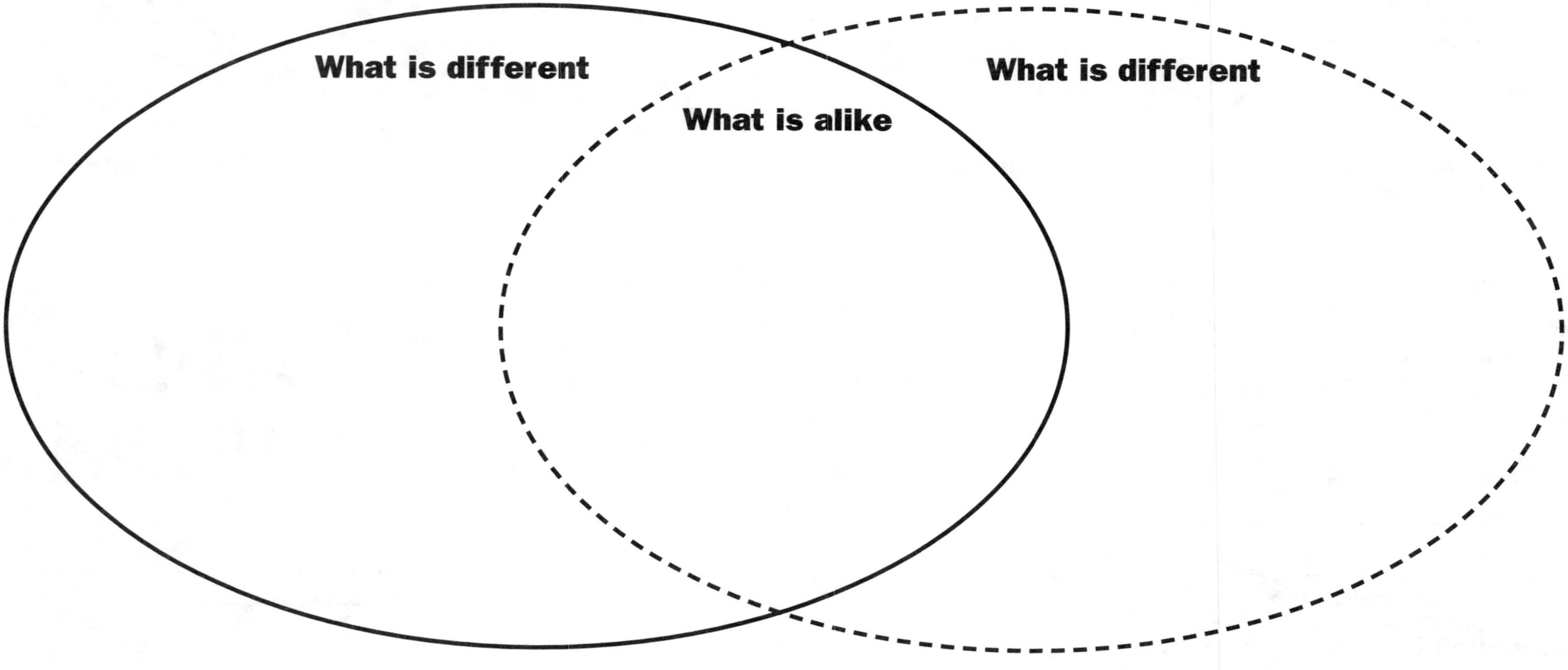

What is different

What is alike

What is different

Name _____

All-Star Book Report

Fill in the lines inside the star. Then follow the directions to fill in each point of the star. Before you know it, you'll have written a 15-word book report! If you want to write more, use the back of this paper.

1. Write 1 word to tell how the story made you feel.

2. Make up a new 2-word title for the story.

5. In just 5 words, tell how the story ended.

3. Name the 3 most important characters in the story.

4. Using 4 words, tell where most of the story took place.

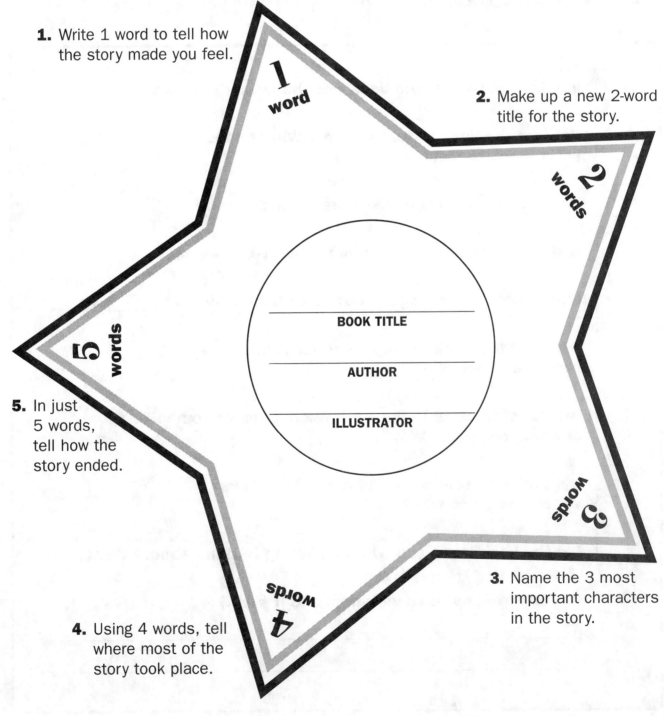

BOOK TITLE

AUTHOR

ILLUSTRATOR

1 word

2 words

3 words

4 words

5 words

Name _____

Book Review Checklist

Here are questions that will help you write a great book review. One important question is already checked for you. Pick at least three more questions to answer in your review. Put a check next to the questions you will answer. Write your answers on a separate sheet of paper. Use those answers when you are writing your review. Remember, you don't have to answer all of these questions.

- ✔ **What is the title of the book and the author's name?**

- ☐ **How did the book make you feel? What happened in the book to make you feel that way?**

- ☐ **Why did you like (or dislike) the main character?**

- ☐ **If there is artwork, did you like it? Why or why not?**

- ☐ **What would you change about this book? Why?**

- ☐ **What did the book teach you about yourself or about someone else?**

- ☐ **Did the characters in the book remind you of yourself or of anyone else? Why?**

- ☐ **Did this book remind you of any other books. Which ones, and why?**

- ☐ **Did the book leave you with something to think about? What?**

- ☐ **(If you have your own question, add it here.)**

_____

_____